The **AA** POCKE

FLORENCE
& TUSCANY

Florence & Tuscany: Regions and Best places to see

Original text by Tim Jepson
Updated by Tim Jepson

© AA Media Limited 2008
First published 2008
Reprinted Aug 2009, Apr 2010

ISBN: 978-0-7495-5536-8

Published by AA Publishing, a trading name of AA Media Limited, whose registered
office is Fanum House, Basing View, Basingstoke, Hampshire RG21 4EA. Registered
number 06112600.

Colour separation: Keenes, Andover
Printed and bound in Italy by Printer Trento S.r.l.

Front cover images: (t) AA/K Paterson; (b) AA/C Sawyer
Back cover image: AA/K Paterson

A04378
Maps in this title produced from mapping © MAIRDUMONT/Falk Verlag 2010
Transport map © Communicarta Ltd, UK

About this book

This book is divided into four sections.

Planning pages 6–19
Before you go; Getting there; Getting around; Being there

Best places to see pages 20–41
The unmissable highlights

Exploring pages 42–127
The best places to visit in Florence and Tuscany, organized by area

Maps pages 131–144
All map references are to the atlas section. For example, the Ponte Vecchio has the reference ➕ 141 D5 indicating the page number and grid square in which it is to be found

Contents

INDEX & ACKNOWLEDGEMENTS

MAPS

Planning

Before you go

WHEN TO GO

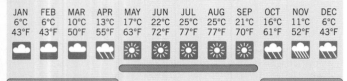

JAN	FEB	MAR	APR	MAY	JUN	JUL	AUG	SEP	OCT	NOV	DEC
6°C	6°C	10°C	13°C	17°C	22°C	25°C	25°C	21°C	16°C	11°C	6°C
43°F	43°F	50°F	55°F	63°F	72°F	77°F	77°F	70°F	61°F	52°F	43°F

⬤ High season   ⬤ Low season

The best times to visit Florence (Firenze) are late March to early June and mid-September to mid-November, when the weather is generally fine but not too hot. Avoid July and August, when the city is not only stifling and uncomfortable, but also extremely crowded. August can also be humid and thunderstorms are possible in summer and through September and October. Winters are short but can be cold, notably in January and February, though these two months are also the quietest periods of the year. Snow is rare. The Tuscan countryside is at its best in spring, from around late March to late May, later in the mountains. Note that the city is also busy around Easter and major religious holidays or events and during school holidays.

WHAT YOU NEED

					UK	Germany	USA	Netherlands	Spain
⬤	Required	Some countries require a passport to remain valid for a minimum period (usually at least six months) beyond the date of entry – check before you travel.							
○	Suggested								
▲	Not required								
Passport (or National Identity Card where applicable)					⬤	⬤	⬤	⬤	⬤
Visa (regulations can change – check before you travel)					▲	▲	▲	▲	▲
Onward or Return Ticket					▲	▲	▲	▲	▲
Health Inoculations					▲	▲	▲	▲	▲
Health Documentation (▶ 9, Health Insurance)					⬤	⬤	▲	⬤	⬤
Travel Insurance					○	○	○	○	○
Driving Licence (national)					⬤	⬤	⬤	⬤	⬤
Car Insurance Certificate (if own car)					○	○	○	○	○
Car Registration Document (if own car)					⬤	⬤	⬤	⬤	⬤

WEBSITES

www.initaly.com
www.italyheaven.co.uk
www.turismo.toscana.it

www.firenze.net
www.comune.firenze.it
www.italiantourism.com

TOURIST OFFICES AT HOME

In the UK

Italian State Tourist Board
1 Princes Street, London W1R 8AY
☎ 020 7408 1254
www.italiantouristboard.co.uk;
www.enit.it

In the USA

Italian Government Travel Office
(ENIT)

630 Fifth Avenue, Suite 1565,
Rockefeller Center, New York NY
10111
☎ 212/245 4822

Italian Government Travel Office
(ENIT)
12400 Wilshire Boulevard, Suite
550, Los Angeles, CA 90025
☎ 310/820 1898

HEALTH INSURANCE

Nationals of EU countries receive medical treatment at reduced cost
and pay a percentage of prescribed medicines. Hospital treatment is at
reduced cost. You need a qualifying document (EHIC – European Health
Insurance Card). However, private medical insurance is advised for all.

Nationals of EU countries can obtain dental treatment at reduced cost
from dentists who operate within the Italian health service. A qualifying
document (EHIC) is needed. Again, private medical insurance is advised
for all.

TIME DIFFERENCES

| GMT | Italy | Germany | USA (NY) | Netherlands | Spain |
| 12 noon | 1PM | 1PM | 7AM | 1PM | 1PM |

Italy is one hour ahead of Greenwich Mean Time (GMT+1), but from late
March, when clocks are put forward one hour, to late September, Italian
Summer Time (GMT+2) operates.

NATIONAL HOLIDAYS

1 Jan New *Year's Day*
6 Jan *Epiphany*
Mar/Apr *Easter Sunday and Monday*
25 Apr *Liberation Day, 1945*
1 May *Labour Day*
15 Aug *Assumption of the Virgin*

1 Nov *All Saints' Day*
8 Dec *Immaculate Conception*
25 Dec *Christmas Day*
26 Dec *St Stephen's Day*

Banks, businesses and most shops and museums are closed on these days, and the road and rail networks are usually very busy.

Florence celebrates its patron saint (St John the Baptist) on 24 June, but most places stay open.

WHAT'S ON WHEN

January *Pitti Immagine:* Florence fashion shows.

February Carnival celebrations across Tuscany, notably processions in Viareggio and San Gimignano (Shrove Tuesday and adjacent weekends).

March *Festa dell'Annunziata:* fair in Florence's Piazza Santissima Annunziata (25th).

April Lucca's summer Sagra Musicale (Music Festival) begins.
Holy Week celebrations many towns and villages
Mostra dell'Artigianato (Florence): international exhibition of crafts and artisans' work (last week).
Scoppo del Carro

(Explosion of the Cart): Easter Sunday service in Florence's Duomo followed by special fireworks.

May *Festa del Grillo:* crickets are sold and released in Florence's Cascine park (Sun after Ascension).
Maggio Musicale (Florence): international festival of music and dance.
Pisa's 'Historic Regatta of the Maritime Republics' (May–end Jun).

June Start of summer arts and music festival in San Gimignano.
Luminaria di San Ranieri: fireworks and illuminated streets in Pisa followed the next day by a historic regatta.
Calcio in Costume: medieval soccer match in Florence
Il Gioco del Ponte: Pisa's costumed 'Battle of the Bridge' (last Sun).
Estate Fiesolana: arts and musical festival in Fiesole.

July *Corso del Palio:* world-famous horse race in Siena's main square (2nd).
Festa di San Paolino (Lucca): crossbow contest and procession.
Opera festival at Barga near Lucca (second half).

August *Cantiere Internazionale* (Montepulciano): festival of contemporary music and dance (first half).
Montepulciano food festival (second Sun).
Corso del Palio: second horse race in Siena's main square (16th).
Luminaria di Santa Croce (Lucca): torchlit procession.
Bravio delle Botti: (Montepulciano): barrel-rolling contest through the streets (last Sun).
International festival of choral music in Arezzo (last two weeks).
Festival Pucciniano: month-long outdoor festival of Puccini's music at Torre del Lago (near Lucca).
Settimana Musicale Senese: week-long music festival in Siena (last week).

September *Festa delle Rificolone* (Florence): torchlit procession
Giostro del Saracino (Arezzo): jousting contest in medieval costume (first Sun).
Wine festivals across the region, notably Greve.

October Florence opera and classical music season, the Teatro Comunale.

Getting there

BY AIR

Pisa (Galileo Galilei) Airport	🚆 5 minutes
	🚌 4 minutes
2km (1.25 miles) to city centre	🚗 10 minutes
Florence Perétola Airport	🚆 N/A
	🚌 10 minutes
5km (3 miles) to city centre	🚗 30 minutes

The main entry into Tuscany is Pisa (Galileo Galilei) Airport (☎ 050/500 707; www.pisa-airport.com), though flights serve Perétola, close to Florence (☎ 055/315 874; www.safnet.it). There is a direct rail link between Florence and Pisa Airport (journey time 1 hour).

BY TRAIN

Two major railway lines serve Tuscany, both of which carry sleeper and other international train services. The first links Florence's main Santa Maria Novella train station to Bologna to the north and Rome to the south. Trains run on this line from France, Switzerland, Germany, Austria and elsewhere. The second runs down the Tuscan coast, connecting Pisa, Livorno and other Tuscan towns and cities to Rome to the south and Genoa and the French Riviera to the north.

BY CAR

Florence lies close to Italy's main autostrada (motoway), the A1, which provides the main approach to the city from Bologna and the north and Rome and the south. On the coast, the A12 provides the main links to Pisa, which is connected in turn to Florence by the A11. Note that tolls are payable on Italian motorways.

BY BUS

Eurolines (0870 514 3219 in the UK, 055 357 110 in Italy; www.eurolines.com) provides long-distance buses to Florence and Siena from the UK and elsewhere, but the services are much slower and often no cheaper than flights or train services. Most long-distance bus services run to the bus station just to the west of the main Santa Maria Novella train station.

BY BOAT

Ferries and cruises ships dock on the Tuscan coast at Livorno, with services to and from Corsica, Sardinia, southern France and elsewhere. Local ferries also link the Tuscan mainland with Elba, Capraia and the other islands of the Tuscan archipelago. Ferries also operate between Porto Santo Stefano and other points on the Argentario peninsula near Orbetello to the islands of Giglio and Giannutri.

Getting around

PUBLIC TRANSPORT

Internal flights Services throughout the country are provided by Alitalia – the national airline (☎ 06/65 621 or 65 643; www.alitalia.it) and smaller companies such as Meridiana, which flies to Perétola airport. Flights to Florence from Rome are 75 minutes; Milan 60 minutes.

Trains Italian State Railways (Trenitalia; www.trenitalia.it) provides a well-run and inexpensive service. Florence is the hub of the Tuscan rail network with good connections with Pisa, Arezzo, Lucca and Viaréggio. The train is more comfortable than a bus but less frequent. There are two classes of travel: first and second.

Regional buses There is no national bus company, though Lazzi (☎ 055/351 061; www.lazzi.it) and SITA (☎ 055/294 955; www.sita-on-line.it) both have a major presence in Tuscany. Bus terminals in larger towns are often next to the rail station; in smaller towns and villages most buses pull in at the central piazza.

Ferries Tuscany has three main ferry ports: Livorno serves Corsica, Sardinia, Sicily and the Tuscan Archipelago. Piombino has services to Elba, connecting to Portoferraio and Corsica, plus the smaller ports of Cavo and Rio Marina. Porto Santo Stefano has ferries to Corsica and Giglio.

Urban transport City buses are inexpensive charging a flat fare. Invariably you need a ticket before getting on. Buy them in tabacchi or from kiosks at bus terminals and stops. In Florence most routes pass by the station. Validate tickets on boarding. The service is reasonably frequent, but buses can get very crowded in rush hours.

TAXIS

Taxis are available in all towns and tourist resorts. Taxis can be hailed, though you will be lucky to find one passing when you want one. Otherwise find a taxi stand (usually at stations and major piazze), or call a radio taxi (in Florence ☎ 055/4390 or 055/4798).

DRIVING

- The Italians drive on the right side of the road.
- Seat belts must be worn in front seats at all times and in rear seats where fitted.
- Random breath-testing takes place. Never drive under the influence of alcohol.
- Fuel is more expensive in Italy than in Britain and most other European countries, but diesel tends to be slightly less expensive. All except garages in rural places sell unleaded fuel *(senza piombo)*. Outside urban areas fuel stations usually open 7am to 12:30pm and 3 to 7:30pm. Credit cards are rarely accepted.
- Speed limits are as follows:
  Toll-operated motorways *(autostrade)*: 130kph (80mph); main roads: 110kph (68mph); secondary roads: 90kph (55mph); urban roads: 50kph (31mph).
- In the event of a breakdown, call 116, giving your registration number and type of car and the nearest ACI (Automobile Club d'Italia) office will assist you. You will be towed to the nearest ACI garage. This service is free to foreign-registered vehicles or cars rented from Rome or Milan airport (you will need to produce your passport).

CAR RENTAL

Car rental is available in most cities and resorts from international and Italian companies but is expensive. Generally small local firms offer better rates but cars can only be reserved locally. Air or train travellers can take advantage of special inclusive deals.

FARES AND CONCESSIONS

Holders of an International Student Identity Card (ISIC) can take advantage of discounts offered to travelling students. Those under 26 who are not students can obtain an International Youth Card from student organizations that entitles the holder to discounts on transport, accommodation and museums. Citizens aged over 60 (and under 18) of EU and a number of other countries with which Italy has a reciprocal arrangement (not including USA) may gain free admission to communal and state museums and receive discounts at other museums and on public transport on production of their passport.

Being there

TOURIST OFFICES

Florence Tourist Offices
Via Cavour 1r
Firenze (Florence)
☎ 055/290 832
www.firenzeturismo.it

Borgo Santa Croce 29r
Firenze (Florence)
☎ 055/234 0444

Piazza della Stazione 4/A
Firenze (Florence)
☎ 055/212 245

Other Tourist Offices
Piazza della Repubblica 28
Arezzo
☎ 0575/377 678

Via Nazionale 42
Visitors & Convention Cortona
☎ 0575/630 352

Piazzale Giuseppe Verdi
Lucca
☎ 0583/442 944

Piazza del Duomo 1
Pisa
☎ 050/560 464

Piazza del Duomo 4
Pistoia
☎ 0573/21 622

Piazza del Duomo
San Gimignano
☎ 0577/940 008

Piazza del Campo 56
Siena
☎ 0577/280 551

Viale G Carducci 10
Viareggio
☎ 0584/962 233

MONEY
The euro (€) is the official currency of Italy. Banknotes are issued in denominations of 5, 10, 20, 50, 100, 200 and 500 euros; coins in denominations of 1, 2, 5, 10, 20 and 50 cents, and 1 and 2 euros.

ELECTRICITY
The power supply is 220 volts. Round two- or three-hole sockets taking plugs of two round pins or sometimes three pins in a vertical row. British visitors should bring an adaptor; US visitors a voltage transformer.

TIPS/GRATUITIES

Yes ✓   No ✕

Hotels (if service included)	✓	10–15%
Restaurants (if service not included)	✓	10–15%
Cafés/bars (if service not included)	✓	€1 minimum
Taxis	✓	15%
Porters	✓	€1
Chambermaids	✓	€2 weekly
Toilet attendants	✓	10 cents min

POSTAL SERVICES

The Italian postal system can be notoriously slow. In Florence the central post office is at Via Pelliceria 8. Post offices in cities and major towns open 8am to 6pm (12:30pm Sat), other offices open Mon–Fri 8:15–7, Sat 8:15–12:30pm. Closed Sun ☎ 055/218 156; www.poste.it

TELEPHONES

Almost every bar in Italy has a telephone, plus there are many in public places. Tokens and phonecards are available from Telecom Italia offices, tobacconists, stations and other outlets.

International dialling codes

From Italy to:

UK: 00 44

Germany: 00 49

USA: 00 1

Netherlands: 00 31

Spain: 00 34

Emergency telephone numbers

Police: 112

Fire: 115

Ambulance: 113

Road Assistance (ACI): 116

EMBASSIES AND CONSULATES

UK ☎ 055/284 133 (Florence)

Germany ☎ 055/294 722 (Florence)

USA ☎ 055/266 951 (Florence)

Netherlands ☎ 055/475 249 (Florence)

Spain ☎ 06 687 1574 (Rome)

HEALTH ADVICE

Sun advice You can get sunburned surprisingly quickly, even through cloud cover, so a sunscreen is recommended at all times.

Drugs Pharmacies *(farmacia)*, recognized by their green cross sign, possess highly trained staff able to offer medical advice on minor ailments and provide a wide range of prescribed and non-prescribed medicines and drugs.

Safe water It is quite safe to drink tap water and water from drinking fountains, but never drink from a tap marked *acqua non potabile*. However, many Italians prefer the taste of bottled mineral water, which is widely available.

PERSONAL SAFETY

The *Carabinieri* (military-style) uniforms and white shoulder belts) deal with general crime and public order. Tuscans are law-abiding. Petty theft is the main problem (bag-snatching, pickpocketing and car break-ins). Some precautions:

● Carry shoulder bags not *on* your shoulder but slung *across* your body.
● Scooter-borne bag-snatchers can be foiled if you keep well away from the edge of the road.
● Do not put anything down on a café or restaurant table.
● Lock car doors and never keep valuables in your car.

OPENING HOURS

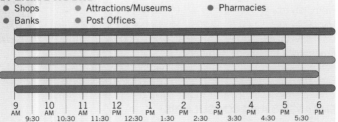

● Shops   ● Attractions/Museums   ● Pharmacies
● Banks   ● Post Offices

| 9 AM | 10 AM | 11 AM | 12 PM | 1 PM | 2 PM | 3 PM | 4 PM | 5 PM | 6 PM |

9:30 10:30 11:30 12:30 1:30 2:30 3:30 4:30 5:30

In addition to the times shown above, some shops are closed Monday morning, others on Saturday afternoon or all day Saturday. Nearly all shops close Sunday, except in Florence and major tourist resorts. Bank afternoon opening times vary but all are closed weekends. Museum times also vary – smaller museums tend to open only in the morning (9am to 1/2pm) and have restricted winter hours. Museums often close early on Sunday (around noon) and most close Monday.

LANGUAGE

The Tuscan dialect is the purest form of spoken Italian. Many Italians speak English, but you will be better received if you at least attempt to communicate in Italian. Italian words are pronounced phonetically. Every vowel and consonant (except 'h') is sounded. The accent usually (but not always) falls on the penultimate syllable. Below is a list of a few words that may be helpful. More extensive coverage can be found in the AA's *Essential Italian Phrase Book*, which lists 2,000 phrases and 2,000 words.

yes	*sì*	help!	*aiuto!*
no	*no*	today	*oggi*
please	*per favore*	tomorrow	*domani*
thank you	*grazie*	yesterday	*ieri*
hello	*ciao*	how much?	*quanto?*
goodbye	*arrivederci*	expensive	*caro*
goodnight	*buona notte*	open	*aperto*
sorry	*mi dispiace*	closed	*chiuso*
hotel	*albergo*	reservation	*prenotazione*
room	*camera*	rate	*tariffa*
..single/double	*..singola/doppia*	breakfast	*prima colazione*
..one/two nights	*per una/due notte/i*	toilet/bath/shower	*toilette/bagno/doccia*
..one/two people	*..per una/due persona/e*	key	*chiave*
restaurant	*ristorante*	lunch	*pranzo/colazione*
café	*caffè*	dinner	*cena*
table	*tavolo*	starter	*il primo*
menu	*menù/carta*	main course	*il secondo*
set menu	*menù turistico*	dish of the day	*piatto del giorno*
wine list	*lista dei vini*	dessert	*dolci*
aeroplane	*aeroplano*	ferry	*traghetto*
airport	*aeroporto*	ticket	*biglietto*
train	*treno*	ticket office	*biglietteria*
bus	*autobus*	timetable	*orario*

Best places to see

1 Cappelle Medicee

The Medici's private chapels and mausoleum feature several of Michelangelo's most outstanding pieces of Florentine funerary sculpture.

The Medici Chapels consist of the Crypt, a mausoleum for minor members of the Medici; the Cappella dei Principi, a vast and opulent chapel dedicated to six of the Medici Grand Dukes; and the Sagrestia Nuova, the last resting place of four of the family's leading lights.

The Crypt is the least interesting area, its dour, low-ceilinged vaults dotted with the brass-railed tombs of 49 lesser Medici. All were buried pell-mell in 1791 by Ferdinand III, only to be exhumed and re-buried in a more dignified manner in 1857. Steps lead from here to the Cappella dei Principi, begun as a family mausoleum for Cosimo I in 1604. A riot of decoration, this vast, marble-lined chapel was the most expensive project ever commissioned by the Medici. Around the walls, 16 coats of arms represent Medici-controlled Tuscan towns.

A corridor leads to the Sagrestia Nuova (New Sacristy), designed as a contrast to Brunelleschi's Old Sacristy in nearby San Lorenzo. It contains three groups of sculpture (1520–34), two wholly and one partly by Michelangelo. On the left is the

tomb of Lorenzo, grandson of Lorenzo the Magnificent, whose statue symbolizes the contemplative life. On the right stands the tomb of Giuliano, third son of Lorenzo the Magnificent, symbolizing the active life. The third (unfinished) group – a Madonna and Child – was intended as the tomb of Lorenzo the Magnificent and his brother Giuliano.

✚ 140 B4 ✉ Piazza Madonna degli Aldobrandini, Florence ☎ 055/238 8602; advance reservation 055/294 883 🕐 Tue–Sun 8:15–1:50 (also 2nd and 4th Mon of month). Closed 2nd and 4th Sun of month 🖐 Expensive 🚍 In the pedestrian zone: nearest service 1, 6, 7 ❓ Visit in conjunction with San Lorenzo (➤ 80–82)

2 Collegiata di San Gimignano

A series of superbly preserved medieval frescoes almost completely covers San Gimignano's most important church.

Most people visit San Gimignano for its 13 famous medieval towers (► 114–115), only to find that the most memorable part of their visit is the fresco-covered Collegiata, a church which served as the village's cathedral until San Gimignano ceased to be a bishopric. Begun in 1148, but later enlarged, it has little in its simple Romanesque façade to prepare you for the decorative wonder inside. Tuscany is filled with fresco cycles, and those in the Collegiata

HOC·OPVS·FIERI·FECIT·IVLIANVS·QVONDAM·AI
MARTINI·CETTI·DE·SCO·GEMINIANO·MCCCC·LXXX

are not necessarily the region's most famous, but few cycles are as extensive, and few have the charm of these. The first panels, by Taddeo di Bartolo, fill the church's back wall and depict the *Last Judgement* (1393), with Paradise and Hell portrayed on two adjoining walls. Below is a large St Sebastian by Benozzo Gozzoli (1420–97).

On the church's right-hand (south) wall is a 22-panel cycle attributed to Lippo Memmi, a 14th-century Sienese artist, which depicts various New Testament scenes from the Passion and the Life of Christ. On the opposite wall are 26 panels (1367) by Bartolo di Fredi, a cycle of Old Testament episodes including scenes from the stories of Genesis, Abraham, Joseph, Moses and Job. To the left of the high altar, the Cappella di San Gimignano has a fine altar (1475) by Benedetto da Maiano, the sculptor who was responsible for the altar, marble shrine and bas-reliefs in the Cappella di Santa Fina (top of the right aisle). This chapel, however, is better known for its fresco cycle by Domenico Ghirlandaio (1449–94), another artist whose work reflects the tone and life of his own period. This cycle depicts the Life of St Fina, one of San Gimignano's patron saints. Look for the fresco which features a 15th-century view of the town.

➕ 137 B7 ✉ Piazza del Duomo 1, San Gimignano ☎ 0577/940 316 🕐 Church and Cappella di Santa Fina: Apr–Oct Mon–Fri 9:30–7:10, Sat 9:30–5:10, Sun 12:30–5:10; Mar, Nov to mid-Jan Mon–Sat 9:30–4:40, Sun 12:30–4:40; mid-Jan to Feb closed except for servies. Check with tourist office 🖐 Moderate 🍴 In Piazza della Cisterna (€–€€) 🚻 In the pedestrian zone

3 *David*

Michelangelo's celebrated statue is one of the most familiar of all Renaissance images, and one of the essential sights of any visit to Florence.

Michelangelo's *David* is exhibited in the Galleria dell'Accademia, Europe's first artistic academy (founded in 1563), together with five other Michelangelo statues and an interesting collection of Gothic and Renaissance paintings. Italy's most famous sculpture was commissioned by the Opera del Duomo in 1501 when Michelangelo was just 26. Its theme – David defeating the tyrant Goliath – was chosen to symbolize the virtues of Florence (then a republic), its freedom from papal and foreign domination, and its recent liberation from Savonarola and the Medici. The marble from

which it was sculpted, a vast 5m (16ft) block, had been quarried from Carrara some 40 years earlier but was so thin and riddled with cracks that it had defied the ambitions of all other sculptors. In Michelangelo's hands however, it was transformed in just three years into a work that secured his reputation as the foremost sculptor of his day.

When it was completed 30 leading artists were asked to select a site for the statue. The Piazza della Signoria was their eventual choice. There *David* remained, ravaged by wind and rain, until 1873. The fact that the figure was intended as a piece of outdoor sculpture helps to explain its famous distortions – notably the over-large hands and face – features designed to emphasise its monumentality.

Elsewhere in the gallery are Michelangelo's *St Matthew* (1504–8) and four unfinished *Slaves*, or *Prisoners* (1521–3), the latter a graphic illustration of Michelangelo's dictum that sculpture was the liberation of a form which was already 'imprisoned' in the stone. There are also paintings by such masters as Botticelli, Perugino, Pontormo, Filippino Lippi and others.

✚ 141 A6 ✉ Via Ricasoli 60, Florence ☎ 055/238 8609; advance reservation 055/294 883 🕐 Tue–Sun 8:15–6:20 ✋ Expensive 🍴 In Piazza San Marco and Via del Ricasoli (€) 🚌 1, 6, 7, 11 and other services to San Marco

Duomo di Siena

This magnificent Gothic cathedral has one of Italy's loveliest façades and an interior bursting with outstanding works of art.

Siena's cathedral was begun in 1196 and completed in 1376, during which time there was an aborted attempt to extend the building, a scheme whose half-finished results can be seen in the skeletal shell to the right of the present structure. Much of the lower part of the façade (1285) was designed by Giovanni Pisano, though most of his original statuary is now in the nearby Museo dell'Opera.

The exterior's distinctive black-and-white banding is echoed in the interior's monochrome floor, which consists of 56 panels (1349–1547) created over the centuries by some of Siena's leading artists. Midway down the left aisle (fourth altar) stands the Piccolomini altar, whose four lower-niche statues are early works by Michelangelo. Alongside lies the entrance to the Libreria Piccolomini, beautifully frescoed by Pinturicchio with scenes from the life of Aeneas Piccolomini (1509), a Tuscan nobleman who became Pope Pius II.

At the end of the left aisle stands the Duomo's masterpiece: Nicola Pisano's Gothic pulpit (1268). To its left, in the corner chapel, is Tino da Camaino's influential Tomb of Cardinal Petroni (1318). Below it lies Donatello's bronze floor tomb of Bishop Pecci (1426). The circular Cappella di San Giovanni in the left transept has a bronze statue of John the Baptist by Donatello and more Pinturicchio frescoes. A similar chapel in the opposite transept, the Cappella Chigi, was designed by Bernini. Be sure to visit the Baptistery, to the rear of the cathedral, which

features swathes of lovely 15th-century frescoes
and a font with bronze panels by Ghiberti, Donatello
and Jacopo della Quercia.

➕ 138 C3 ✉ Piazza del Duomo, Siena ☎ 0577/283 048
🕙 Duomo: Mar–late Aug Mon–Sat 10:30–7:30, Sun
1:30–7:30; late Aug–late Oct daily 9:30–7:30; late Oct–Feb
Mon–Sat 10:30–6:30, Sun 1:30–6:30 ✋ Duomo:
inexpensive (includes Libreria Piccolomini). Baptistery:
inexpensive. Duomo: expensive late Aug–late Oct 🚌 In the
pedestrian zone: occasional shuttle bus services

5 Galleria degli Uffizi

One of the world's finest art galleries, the Uffizi contains a collection of paintings that features all the great names of the Florentine Renaissance.

The building housing the Uffizi was begun by Vasari in 1560, its original purpose being to serve as a suite of offices *(uffizi)* from which the Medici could administer the Grand Duchy of Tuscany. In 1737 it was bequeathed to Florence, along with the Medici art collection, by Anna Luisa, sister of Gian Gastone, the last Medici Grand Duke. Today its 45 rooms house not only the cream of 14th- and 15th-century Florentine paintings, but also masterpieces from elsewhere in Italy (notably Venice and Siena), together with a surprising

number of major works from Germany, Holland and Spain. Rooms 1–15 are given over to the Florentine Renaissance (and contain the most famous paintings); rooms 16–27 concentrate on the age of High Renaissance and Mannerism, and rooms 28–45 are devoted to later Italian and European paintings.

Highlights are too numerous to mention, though certain works deserve extra special attention. Room 2 opens with altarpieces of the *Maestà (Madonna Enthroned)* by Giotto, Duccio and Cimabue, three of Italy's greatest 13th-century painters, who contributed to the

movement towards naturalism and emotion and away from the stilted and more stylized Byzantine approach to subjects in art. Room 3's Sienese paintings are dominated by Simone Martini's sublime *Annunciation*, while in rooms 5 and 6 the key work is Gentile da Fabriano's exquisitely detailed *Adoration of the Magi*. Rooms 10–14 feature paintings by Botticelli, notably the famous *Primavera* and *Birth of Venus*. Room 18 is best known for the *Venus de' Medici*, renowned for centuries as one of antiquity's most erotic statues. Successive rooms feature works by, among others, Raphael, Caravaggio and Michelangelo; the Venetians Titian, Giorgione and Carpaccio; and Europeans such as Rembrandt, Rubens and Van Dyck.

➕ 141 E5 ✉ Loggiato degli Uffizi 6, off Piazza della Signoria, Florence ☎ 055/238 8651 🕐 Tue–Sun 8:15–6:50 (ticket office closes 45 mins earlier). Closed Mon, 1 Jan, Easter Sun, 1 May, 15 Aug, 25 Dec 🖐 Expensive 🍽 Café (€) 🚌 In the pedestrian zone ❓ Tickets can be reserved for admission at a set time to the Uffizi and other museums by calling Firenze Musei 055/294 883

6 Museo Nazionale del Bargello

Italy's greatest collection of Renaissance sculpture is contained in the Bargello, together with an array of majolica, tapestries, paintings and silverware.

The fortress-like Bargello, begun in 1255, was Florence's earliest civic palace, serving first as the city's seat of government and later as the home of the chief of police. Later still it became a prison, torture chamber and place of execution, assuming its present role in 1865. The museum spreads over three floors, though its key works are found in just two large rooms. The first lies to the right of the

ticket hall, and concentrates on the late Renaissance works of Michelangelo, Giambologna and Benvenuto Cellini. Michelangelo is represented by three contrasting works: a delicate tondo (circular artwork) of the Madonna and Child; a powerful portrait bust of Brutus; and a lurching, soft-bellied statue of Bacchus. Other highlights include a bronze of Cosimo I by Cellini and Giambologna's celebrated Mercury, a sublime study in speed.

From this first room, wander into the courtyard, glance at the exterior sculptures in the small rooms opposite, and then climb the external staircase to the first floor. At the top of the stairs is a wonderful menagerie of bronze animals by Giambologna. Turn right and you come to the museum's second major room, a glorious vaulted hall filled with sculptural masterpieces. Look in particular for the works of Donatello, notably his St George, removed from Orsanmichele; the Marzocco, Florence's heraldic lion; and the debonair and famously androgynous statue of David. Subsequent rooms are crammed with all manner of interesting rugs, tapestries, glassware, silverware and many other precious objets d'art. Particularly noteworthy is the Salone del Camino, which contains Italy's most important collection of small bronzes.

✚ 141 D6 ✉ Via del Proconsolo 4, Florence ☎ 055/238 8606; advance reservation 055/294 883 🕐 Tue–Sun 8:15–1:50. Closed 1st, 3rd, 5th Sun and 2nd, 4th Mon of month 👖 Moderate 🍴 Via del Proconsolo (€) 🚌 19

7 Museo di San Marco

The ancient Dominican convent of San Marco is renowned for a series of sublime frescoes and paintings by Fra Angelico.

San Marco was originally owned by Vallombrosan and Sylvestrine monks, passing to the Dominicans in 1436, when it was restored at Cosimo de' Medici's personal expense. Its subsequent priors included Fra Angelico, not only a devout Dominican, but also one of the finest of Florence's early Renaissance painters. Today the convent buildings are a museum given over almost entirely to the artist's paintings and frescoes.

Many of the paintings are contained in the Ospizio dei Pellegrini, a room once used to provide pilgrims with food and shelter (located off the main cloister). Its two masterpieces hang on opposite walls: a Deposition (1440), removed from the church of Santa Trínita, and the Madonna dei Linaiuoli (1433), commissioned for the headquarters of the flax-makers' *(linaiuoli)* guild. Also off the cloister is the Sala Capitolare, or Chapter House, which features a Crucifixion (1442) by Fra Angelico. The Refectory nearby contains a large fresco of the Last Supper by Domenico Ghirlandaio (beyond the shop).

Steps from the cloister lead to the first floor, where you are greeted by Fra Angelico's famous *Annunciation* (c.1445), one of the most beautiful of all Renaissance paintings. The rest of the floor is largely taken up by 44 dormitory cells, each

frescoed by Fra Angelico and his pupils with religious scenes intended as aids to monastic devotion. At the end of the far corridor are three cells once occupied by Savonarola. At the end of the corridor on your right are two cells, larger than the rest, once used by Cosimo il Vecchio de' Medici. Close by is Europe's first public library, designed for Cosimo by Michelozzo in 1441.

✠ 141 A6 ✉ Piazza San Marco, Florence ☎ 055/238 8608; advance reservations 055/294 883 ⏰ Mon–Fri 8:30–1:50, Sat 8:15/30–6:50, Sun 8:15/30–7. Closed 1st, 3rd, 5th Sun and 2nd, 4th Mon of month ✋ Moderate 🍴 In Piazza San Marco (€) 🚌 1, 6, 7, 10, 11, 17, 20, 25, 31, 32, 33

8 Piazza del Campo

Siena's magnificent central piazza and its arc of rosy palaces make up one of Europe's most beautiful medieval squares.

Walking into the Campo from Siena's tight huddle of streets is like stepping on to some medieval stage set. Situated at the heart of the old city, the conch-shaped piazza resembles a vast amphitheatre, its broad sweep of palaces culminating in the battlemented grandeur of the Palazzo Pubblico and its attendant bell tower.

The square probably began life as the Roman forum, becoming the town's principal marketplace before taking on its present form in 1293, when the Council of Nine, Siena's governing body, began to buy up land with a view to creating a great central square. The carefully chosen area was at the heart of Siena's *terzi* (the city's three main districts), and was the only piece of land

owned by none of Siena's *contrade*, the city's fiercely competitive medieval parishes. As such the Council hoped the square would become the focus of civic life, a physical expression of good government, and a symbol of citizens' loyalty to Siena rather than to factions, families, *terzi* or *contrade*.

The Campo was completed in 1349 with the addition of its brick

paving, whose nine sections were designed to symbolize the Council of Nine, and the folds of the Virgin's cloak, sheltering the city under its protective embrace. Both the Palazzo Pubblico and Torre del Mangia are well worth visiting, but you should also indulge in at least one pricey cappuccino at one of the Campo's cafés, an ideal way to take in the square's endless street life. Be warned, however, most of the restaurants are very expensive.

✚ 138 C3 ✉ Piazza del Campo, Siena ☎ None ◷ Daily 24 hours ⚑ Free ⑪ Many cafés (€–€€) and restaurants (€€€) in the square ⊟ In the pedestrian zone

Santa Croce

The most famous church in Florence is celebrated for its superb Giotto frescoes and the tombs of Galileo, Michelangelo and Machiavelli.

Begun in 1294 by Arnolfo di Cambio, and completed in 1450, this Franciscan foundation attracted the attention of many wealthy families, all anxious to seek spiritual salvation by being buried among the 'humble' Franciscans; hence the many tombs and the various frescoed family chapels (notably those of the Bardi, Peruzzi and Baroncelli).

Among those buried in the church are Michelangelo (first tomb on the right), Machiavelli (sixth on the right) and Galileo (first on the left). There are also outstanding examples of Renaissance funerary sculpture, notably 15th-century works by Bernardo Rossellino (end of the right aisle) and Desiderio da Settignano (end of the left aisle). More famous still are the church's fresco cycles, the best known of which are by Giotto, who was responsible for the paintings in the Cappella Bardi and the Cappella Peruzzi (adjacent chapels to the right of the high altar).

To the right of the church lie the Cappella dei Pazzi (1430) and the Museo dell'Opera di Santa Croce. The former, rather austere chapel by Brunelleschi, is simply decorated with 12 terracotta tondi of the Apostles by Luca della Robbia, who also decorated the portico and polychrome roundels in the upper corners (attributed to Brunelleschi and Donatello). The Museo's highlights are Donatello's St Louise of Toulouse and a crucifix by Cimabue.

✚ 141 E7 ✉ Piazza Santa Croce, Florence ☎ 055/246 6105 🕙 Mon–Sat 9:30–5:30, Sun 1–5:30; may open later in summer ✋ Church: moderate; includes Museo dell'Opera di Santa Croce and Cappella dei Pazzi 🍴 In Piazza Santa Croce (€) 🚌 13, 23, shuttle bus B

10 Torre Pendente

Few sights are as immediately recognizable as the Leaning Tower of Pisa, one of several monuments in Pisa's beautiful Campo dei Miracoli.

Pisa's famous Tower was begun in 1173 as a companion for the city's Duomo and Baptistery, two buildings which make up a lovely medieval ensemble in a green-lawned square known as the Campo dei Miracoli ('Field of Miracles'). The tower began to lean almost from the outset, tilting into the sandy subsoil under the foundations (this part of the coast was once under water, so that local soil is composed almost entirely of sand and silt). Initial construction work on the tower was abandoned after only three storeys were complete, but work resumed in the 13th century when it was accepted that the tower would not fall. Over the next 180 years a series of architects tried to correct the lean by adding off-centre sections. None was successful. At its worst, the tower was a dizzying 5.2m (17ft) to the vertical.

Architects agonized over how to prevent the tower's collapse and reverse the lean. Many schemes were put forward, but none was taken seriously until the tower was closed to the public in 1990 after it was deemed to have become dangerous. Over the next few years, some 900 tonnes of lead were strapped to the tower's base on its northern side to help counter the lean. By 1998 some improvement had been seen, and a delicate drilling operation began to remove water and subsoil from the tower's northern foundations. The drying of the soil and the removal of material created a gradual subsidence on one side of the tower, which saw the lean corrected by around 10 per cent, bringing it to the angle it had in 1838. The project cost over £20 million and took 11 years to complete.

132 F4 ✉ Campo (Piazza) dei Miracoli, Pisa ☎ Prebook tours (050/506 547; www.opapisa.it) ⑬ Tours only every 35–40 mins: end Mar–Sep daily 8:30–8:30; 1st two weeks Mar 9–6; 3rd week Mar, Oct 9–7; Nov–Feb 10–5 (9–6 25 Dec–7 Jan). Late opening mid-Jun to 1st week Sep 8:30am–11pm; call to confirm ✋ Tower: expensive 🚌 1 from rail station

Exploring

Florence (Firenze) is one of the world's greatest artistic cities. A focal point for the Renaissance, one of history's most dramatic periods of creative endeavour, its churches, galleries and museums are filled with some of the finest art ever created. This said, not all your time should be spent admiring art. Florence has some superb shopping, from designer names to lively markets, and there are excellent, bars, cafés and restaurants, as well as the simple charm of its medieval and Renaissance streets.

In Tuscany, right on its doorstep, is one of Europe's most beautiful regions, a perfect patchwork of historic hill towns – notably Siena, Lucca and San Gimignano – sandy beaches, timeless pastoral countryside, jagged mountain peaks and much more. It provides a perfect escape from the hustle and bustle and, in summer, the sheer heat of Florence.

Florence

Florence is compact and easily explored on foot, though its wealth of art and culture, and the way sights are scattered across the city, make it difficult to plan convenient sightseeing itineraries. The historic heart conforms to the grid of the old Roman colony, its principal points of interest lying on and around two main squares: Piazza del Duomo and Piazza della Signoria.

Most people begin a tour of the city in Piazza del Duomo, where you should see the Duomo (cathedral), Baptistery and Museo dell'Opera, as well as climb the Campanile or cathedral dome for a superb view of the city. Close by lies the Museo Nazionale del Bargello, Italy's greatest collection of Renaissance sculpture. Via dei Calzaiuoli, Florence's pedestrianized main street, leads south to Piazza della Signoria, where you should visit the Palazzo Vecchio, the Uffizi and the nearby Museo di Storia della Scienza.

   North of the central district the key sights are the Cappelle Medicee, with statues by Michelangelo, the Accademia (home to Michelangelo's *David*) and the Palazzo Medici-Riccardi, with its lovely fresco cycle. A little further north lies the Museo di San Marco, filled with sublime paintings by Fra Angelico. The city's two most important churches – Santa Croce and Santa Maria

Novella – lie east and west of the centre respectively. Across the Arno, the river that divides the city, is the quieter Oltrarno district, worth visiting for the Cappella Brancacci and its fresco cycle, and the Palazzo Pitti, home to a superb collection of Medici art and objects.

www.firenzeturismo.it

✚ 134 F3

ℹ Via Cavour 1r ☎ 055/290 832

BATTISTERO

The Baptistery of Florence was long believed to have been a Roman temple to Mars; the disovery of floor fragments has confirmed the existence of a 1st-century palace on the site, though the core of the present building probably dates from the 6th to 7th centuries. The marble decoration of the classically inspired exterior, remodelled in the 11th century, was to inspire generations of architects and provide the model for countless Tuscan churches.

The south doors (1328–36), the work of Andrea Pisano, depict scenes from the life of St John the Baptist (the patron saint of Florence), and were cast by Venetian bell makers, then Europe's most accomplished bronze smiths. A famous competition was arranged in 1401 to award the commission for the north doors (1403–24), an event widely considered to have marked the 'beginning' of the Renaissance. It was won by Lorenzo Ghiberti, also responsible for the east doors (1425–52), works so exquisite they are often known as the 'Gates of Paradise' (the original panels are now in the Museo dell'Opera, ➤ 62–63).

Inside, the highlights are the mosaic ceiling (begun in 1225), created by Venetian mosaicists, and the glorious tessellated marble floor, at whose heart you can still see the outlines of the building's original font (all Florentine children were once baptized here). Less eye-catching are the fine mosaic frieze; the lovely upper gallery and – to the right of the apse, or *scarsella* – the distinctive *Tomb of the Antipope John XXIII* (1427) by Donatello and Michelozzo.

✚ 141 C5 ✉ Piazza San Giovanni, Piazza del Duomo ☎ 055/230 2885 or 294 514 🕐 Mon–Sat 12–7, Sun and religious hols 8:30–1:30. Closed Jan, Easter Sun, 24 Jun, 25–26 Dec ✋ Inexpensive 🚌 1, 6, 7, 11, 14, 23

CAMPANILE

The multihued Campanile is one of Italy's most beautiful bell towers, and the views from its pinnacle are a highlight of any visit to Florence. At 85m (279ft), it is just 6m (20ft) lower than the Duomo, close by, and to reach the summit you have to climb 414 steps (there is no elevator).

Begun in 1334, the tower was probably designed by Giotto, who laboured on the project during his reign as city architect and *capo maestro* (head of works). At his death in 1337, however, only the base – the first of the tower's present five levels – was complete.

Work on the second floor (1337–42) was supervised by Andrea Pisano, fresh from his work on the Baptistery's north doors. When he moved on, responsibility passed to Francesco Talenti, who completed the decoration and the remaining three floors (1348–59).

Most of the Campanile's many reliefs – probably designed by Giotto – are copies; the originals now reside in the Museo dell'Opera. Two sets decorate the first floor, the lower tier in hexagonal frames, the upper tier in diamonds. The hexagonal reliefs, by Pisano and his pupils, depict the Creation, the Arts and Industries and the Seven Sacraments. The Five Liberal Arts (Grammar, Philosophy, Music, Arithmetic and Astronomy) on the northern face are by Luca della Robbia. The upper reliefs, also the work of Pisano, portray the Seven Planets and Seven Virtues. On the second floor, the niche sculptures of the Sibyls and Prophets are copies of works by Donatello and others, now in the Museo dell'Opera.

✚ 141 C5 ✉ Piazza del Duomo ☎ 055/230 2885, 294 514 or 271 071
🕐 Daily 8:30–6:40. Closing times indicate last admission: tower remains open 50 mins thereafter. Closed 1 Jan, Easter Sun, 8 Sep, 25–26 Dec
💷 Expensive 🚌 1, 6, 7, 11, 14, 23

CAPPELLA BRANCACCI

On its own, the church of Santa Maria del Carmine would merit
little attention. Constructed between 1268 and 1422, it was almost
completely rebuilt after a disastrous fire in 1771. One of the areas
that survived the conflagration, however, was the Cappella
Brancacci, a tiny chapel decorated with one of the most important
and influential fresco cycles in Western art. It was commissioned
in 1424 by Felice Brancacci, a former Florentine ambassador to
Egypt, and its decoration entrusted to Masolino da Panicale
(1383–1447) and his young assistant, Tommaso di Ser Giovanni di
Mone Cassai (better known by his nickname Masaccio, or 'Mad

Tom'). In 1426 Masaccio's burgeoning talents were given fuller rein when Masolino was recalled to Budapest where he was employed as a painter to the Hungarian court.

In his absence Masaccio demonstrated a mastery of perspective, narrative drama and bold naturalism not seen in Florence since the days of Giotto. Masolino returned in 1427 but was called away to Rome a year later. Masaccio followed him after a few months, and neither painter worked in the chapel again. Masaccio died in the Holy City in 1428, at only 28 years old. In 1436 Brancacci was exiled by Cosimo de' Medici, leaving the frescoes untouched until their completion by Filippino Lippi in 1485. All but two of the frescoes depict scenes from the Life of St Peter, and all of them are outstanding, but note in particular Masaccio's very powerful panel of *Adam and Eve Banished from Paradise* (top tier, extreme left). It is an excellent illustration of Masaccio's clever employment of stark and angular figures to portray profound emotion.

✚ 140 E1 ✉ Santa Maria del Carmine, Piazza del Carmine ☎ Prebook by phone 055/276 8224 🕐 Mon, Wed–Sat 10–5, Sun and public hols 1–5. Closed Tue, Easter Sun, 25 Dec ✋ Moderate 🚌 Shuttle bus B ❓ Entered via the cloisters of Santa Maria del Carmine (to the right of the church façade)

CAPPELLE MEDICEE
Best places to see, pages 22–23.

CASA BUANAROTTI

The Casa Buonarroti, bought by Michelangelo in 1508, is often described as the sculptor's house (Michelangelo's surname was Buonarroti). In fact the maestro never lived here; the present house, its decoration and its collection of Michelangelo memorabilia were arranged by his nephew Leonardo (his sole descendant), and subsequently by Leonardo's son, Michelangelo the Younger. The house, if a little impersonal, is beautifully presented, its stylish appearance the result of expensive restoration following the 1966 flood. The admission charge is a touch over-priced, however, especially given the fact that the museum contains only four minor works and a handful of drawings by the master. At the same time, the maze of decorated rooms, antique furniture, frescoed ceilings and various *objets d'art* are all attractive in their own right.

The sculptural highlights are on the first floor. The earliest, the *Madonna della Scala* (1491), is a delicate, shallow relief showing the influence of Donatello. Carved when Michelangelo was still in his teens, it is his earliest known work. Nearby stands the *Battle of the Centaurs* (1492), a more complex work executed when Michelangelo was employed by Lorenzo the Magnificent. The adjoining room features a wooden model of Michelangelo's plan for the façade of San Lorenzo (never realized), together with a sprawling wood-and-wax model of a torso, part of a huge river god possibly intended for the Cappelle Medicee. A room to the right contains a slender crucifix, a work believed lost until its discovery in 1965.

✚ 141 D7 ✉ Via Ghibellina 70 ☎ 055/241 752; www.casabuonarroti.it
⊙ Mon, Wed–Sun 9:30–2. Closed Tue, 1 Jan, Easter Sun, 25 April, 1 May, 15 Aug, 25–26 Dec 🎟 Expensive 🚌 13, 19, 23, shuttle bus B

DUOMO (SANTA MARIA DEL FIORE)

The first church on the site of Santa Maria del Fiore, Florence's magnificent cathedral, was built in the 7th century and dedicated to Santa Reparata, an obscure Syrian or Palestinian saint and martyr (San Lorenzo and the Baptistery served as Florence's cathedral for much of the city's early history). In the 13th century, when Florence was a prosperous and sophisticated metropolis, the city's elders declared the old church too 'crudely built and too small for such a city'. They envisaged something to rival the new cathedrals of Siena and Pisa – something, as an edict of 1294 put it, of the 'most exalted and most prodigal magnificence, in order that the industry and power of men may never create or undertake anything whatsoever more vast and more beautiful'.

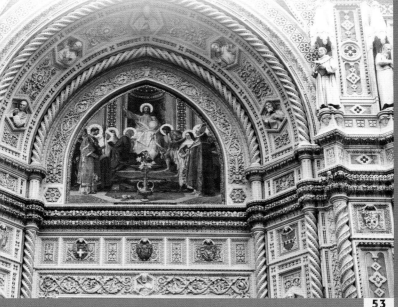

Responsibility for designing this magnificence was entrusted
to Arnolfo di Cambio in 1294. After his death six years later, work
lapsed until 1331; Giotto took over as the building's master of
works in 1334. Construction of the vast Gothic nave, the tribunes
(apses) and the drum of the colossal dome was finally completed
in 1418.

The cathedral's interior is strikingly austere. It is also breathtaking in size – it can accommodate some 10,000 people – and ranks as Europe's fourth largest church after St Peter's and the cathedrals of Milan and St Paul's in London. The highlights include two large frescoed equestrian portraits on the north (left) wall: one of the English mercenary Sir John Hawkwood (1436) by Paolo Uccello, the other of Niccolò da Tolentino (1456) – another soldier of fortune – by Andrea del Castagno. Note, too, the clock above the main door by Paolo Uccello and the *Tomb of Antonio d'Orso* (1323) to its right, the work of Mino da Fiesole. Much of the stained glass in the apses was designed by Lorenzo Ghiberti, as was the superb reliquary (1432–42) in the middle (third) chapel of the central apse.

The cathedral's main highlight, however, is its vast dome, one of the supreme feats of late medieval engineering. Designed by Brunelleschi, who won the commission in 1418, it was built using many innovative techniques which are still shrouded in mystery. The key to the project's success was the construction of an inner and an outer shell, as well as the use of a herringbone pattern of bricks arranged in cantilevered rings (allowing the dome to support itself as it rose). Its interior is decorated with frescoes of the *Last Judgement* (1572–9) by Vasari, much criticized over the centuries as unworthy of so great a building. They pale into insignificance alongside the view from the dome's lantern, which is reached by steps from the top of the north (left) aisle.

✚ 141 C5 ✉ Piazza del Duomo ☎ 055/230 2885, 271 071, 294 514
🕐 Cathedral and crypt Mon–Fri 10–5 (Thu 10–3:30), Sun 1:30–4:45, 1st Sat of the month 10–3:30, otherwise Sat 10–4:45. Dome: Mon–Fri 8:30–6:50, 1st Sat of month 8:30–3:20, otherwise 8:30–5. Closed Sun and public hols
✋ Cathedral: free. Dome: expensive. Crypt: inexpensive 🚌 1, 6, 7, 11, 14, 23

GALLERIA DEGLI UFFIZI

Best places to see, pages 30–31.

GIARDINO DI BOBOLI

Italy's most popular gardens were begun in 1549, when the Medici moved to the nearby Palazzo Pitti. They were opened to the public in 1766. Today they are one of the loveliest places in the city to rest, picnic or take a siesta. They also offer sweeping views of the Florentine skyline, notably from the belvederes (viewpoints) beside the rococo *Kaffeehaus* and the Giardino del Cavaliere. From the Palazzo Pitti's main courtyard, where the gardens are entered, paths lead to the Amphitheatre, a large arena designed to house Medici entertainments (it was built over the quarry used for the Palazzo's building stone). Sightseeing highlights include many antique, Renaissance and Mannerist statues; countless fountains (especially *Ganymede* and *Neptune*); and the Viottolone, a long, statue-lined avenue of cypresses that culminates in the Isolotto, a pretty, moated island garden. The gardens also contain the small Museo delle Porcellane, a collection of antique porcelain, which can be visited on a combined ticket with the gardens and Museo degli Argenti (► 71). Free maps of the garden (in Italian text) are sometimes available on request at the ticket office.

🚩 140 F4 ✉ Piazza dei Pitti ☎ Gardens: 055/265 1838. Museo delle Porcellane: 055/238 8605 🕓 Jun–Aug daily 8:15–7:30; Apr, May, Sep, Oct daily 9–6:30; Mar daily 8:15–6:30; Nov–Feb daily 8:15–4:30. Closed 1st and last Mon in month. Last admission 1 hour before closing. Museo delle Porcellane: same hours as gardens 👆 Gardens: expensive. Museo delle Porcellane: expensive 🍴 Kaffeehaus (summer only) and nearby in Piazza dei Pitti (€) 🚌 11, 36, 37, shuttle buses B, C ❓ Public toilets are in the Palazzo Pitti, at the eastern side of the Amphitheatre and in the Kaffeehaus (summer only)

MUSEO DELLA ANTICA CASA FIORENTINA

This beautiful medieval house offers a wonderful insight into how Florence's artists, merchants and noble families might once have

lived. The house was built in about 1330 for the Davizzi, a family of wealthy wool merchants. It was then sold to the Davanzati, who remained the owners until 1838. It opened as a museum in 1910 and was bought by the state in 1951.

In the entrance courtyard, storerooms to the rear were kept stocked in case of siege or famine, while a private well served the house with water, a luxury in an age when most water was still drawn from

public fountains. The age-old wooden staircase, the only one of its kind in Florence, leads to the first of the three floors, each of which is dotted with beautifully furnished rooms and evocative medieval corners.

Highlights of the first floor include the Sala dei Pappagalli, named after the parrots *(pappagalli)* adorning its frescoes, and the gorgeous Sala Pavoni or Camera Nuziale (Wedding Room). The latter features a glorious 14th-century Sicilian bedspread, a two-winged tabernacle by Neri di Bicci and a lovely frescoed frieze of trees, peacocks *(pavoni)* and exotic birds. The third floor is given over to the delightful palace kitchen, a room often situated on the upper floor of medieval houses to minimize damage in the event of fire.

➕ 140 D4 ✉ Palazzo Davanzati, Via Porta Rossa 13 ☎ 055/238 8610
🕐 Daily 8:15–1:50. Closed 1st, 3rd, 5th Mon and 2nd, 4th Sun of month
✋ Free 🍴 In Piazza della Repubblica (€) 🚌 In the pedestrian zone: nearest services 6, 11, 31, 32, 37 to Piazza Santa Trínita ❓ Parts of the museum are closed for restoration: consult the tourist office for latest details

MUSEO BARDINI

Unjustifiably ignored by most visitors, the Museo Bardini was created by Stefano Bardini, a 19th-century art dealer whose own collection became too large for his home, and was transferred to this ersatz 'palace' created from doors, ceilings and fireplaces salvaged from demolished medieval buildings.

The exhibits are housed in some 20 rooms arranged over two floors. On the ground floor rooms 7 and 8 feature some of the museum's highlights, notably a Cosmati pulpit, a tiny carved head attributed to Nicola Pisano, and a stunning Gothic *aedicule* (canopy) framing a statue of Charity by Tino da Camaino.

The first floor begins with armour and medieval weaponry. Room 14 has two of the collection's treasures: a terracotta *Madonna and Child* and the collage-like *Madonna dei Cordai*, both attributed to Donatello. Successive rooms offer a bewitching miscellany of reliefs, furniture and majolica. Room 20 boasts two magnificently inlaid choir stalls and one of the city's grandest wooden ceilings.

🔶 141 F6 ✉ Piazza de' Mozzi 1 ☎ 055/234 2427
🕐 Temporarily closed 👋 Moderate 🍴 On Lungarno Serristori
(€) 🚌 Shuttle buses B and C

MUSEO DI FIRENZE COM'ERA

This is one of the city's most interesting minor museums, thanks to a collection of paintings, engraving and topographical drawings evoking the

Florence of days gone by. The first room contains its principal treasure, the *Pianta della Catena*, a vast panorama of the city as it appeared in 1470. The room to its right features lunette paintings (1599) of the Medici villas by the Flemish painter van Utens – among the loveliest things in any Florentine museum.

Other highlights include the engravings of Telemaco Signorini (1874) and a vaulted room devoted to drawings and engravings of the city's major buildings.

✚ 141 C6 ✉ Via dell'Oriuolo 24 ☎ 055/261 6545 ◷ Sep–Jun Mon–Wed 9–1:30, Sat 9–6:30; Jul–Aug Mon, Tue 9–1:30, Sat 9–6:30. Note hours are subject to change. Closed Thu, 1 Jan, Easter Sun, 1 May, 15 Aug, 25–26 Dec ✋ Inexpensive 🚌 14, 23, shuttle bus B

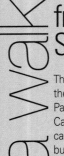

from the Ponte Vecchio to San Miniato al Monte

This mainly uphill walk takes in some of the key sights of the Oltrarno and can easily be extended to embrace the Palazzo Pitti (➤ 70–72), Giardino di Boboli (➤ 56) and Cappella Brancacci (➤ 50–51). As a less strenuous option, it can be walked in reverse, downhill, by catching a 12 or 13 bus to Piazzale Michelangelo or San Miniato al Monte.

Cross the Ponte Vecchio and follow Via de' Guicciardini to Piazza Santa Felicita.

Santa Felicita, probably Florence's second oldest church after San Lorenzo, is noted for Brunelleschi's Cappella Capponi, celebrated in turn for Pontormo's *Deposition* (1525–8), a masterpiece of Mannerist painting.

Take the lane left of the church and turn immediately left to Via de' Bardi. Turn right and follow Via de' Bardi. Continue to Piazza de' Mozzi if you wish to visit the

*Museo Bardini. Otherwise turn right and dogleg up
Costa Scarpuccia. Turn left on Costa di San Giorgio.*

Number 19 Costa di San Giorgio was the home of Galileo.
At the top of the street lies Porta San Giorgio (1258), the
city's oldest surviving gateway. To the right is the entrance
to the Forte di Belvedere (1590–95), built by Buontalenti for
Ferdinand I, with wonderful views from its ramparts.

*At Porta San Giorgio turn right and follow Via di
Belvedere and the city walls for views over olive groves
and the distant hills. At Porta San Miniato and the
crossroads at the bottom turn right. After 150m (164yds)
turn left on the stepped lane of Via di San Salvatore del
Monte. This climbs past Stations of the Cross to Viale
Galileo Galilei.*

Turn left for Piazzale Michelangelo. Turn right; after some
50m (164ft) steps and terraces lead off left to San Miniato
al Monte. The 11th-century marble-clad church is worth a
visit, and the views from here are also good if Piazzale
Michelangelo below is rather crowded.

Distance 2km (1.2 miles)
Time 45 mins or 2–3 hours with visits to churches, Museo Bardini
and Forte del Belvedere
Start point Ponte Vecchio ✚ 141 D5
End point San Miniato al Monte ✚ 141 F6 (off map)
Lunch Cafés and restaurants with views on Viale Galileo Galilei

Santa Felicita
✉ Piazza Santa Felicita ☎ 055/213 018 🕓 Daily 9–12, 3–6 ✋ Free

Forte di Belvedere
✉ Costa di San Giorgio–Via di Belvedere ☎ 055/234 2822 🕓 Daily
9–dusk ✋ Free except during temporary exhibitions

MUSEO NAZIONALE DEL BARGELLO
Best places to see, pages 32–33.

MUSEO DELL'OPERA DEL DUOMO
The Opera del Duomo was established in 1296 to
supervise construction and maintenance of the
cathedral and its many works of art. Today its
sculpture collection ranks second only to the
Bargello, having long housed artefacts removed
for safekeeping from the Duomo, Baptistery and
Campanile. The ground and mezzanine floors
feature rooms filled with tools and models used
during the Duomo's construction, together with
sculpture removed from Arnolfo di Cambio's
unfinished cathedral façade (demolished in 1587).
Highlights from the latter include Donatello's *St
John*, the thickset *Madonna of the Glass Eyes*
and the stiff-backed figure of *Pope Boniface VIII*.
Donatello insisted on having a lock put on his
workshop here after a rival sculptor had sneaked
in to see his work in progress. Other parts of the
museum feature models (1588) for the cathedral
façade (none were ever realized); several
illustrated volumes of choral music; and an
octagonal chapel containing reliquaries and a
lovely 14th-century altarpiece (1334).

The stairs to the upper floors feature
Michelangelo's outstanding *Pietà* (1550), a
fitting prelude to two superlative *cantorie*, or
carved choir lofts, which dominate the floor's
opening room. The loft on the left (1431–8),
carved in white marble, is by Luca della Robbia,
that on the right (1433–9), with a far more
dramatic arrangement by Donatello. The room to

the left features many age-blackened reliefs also from the Campanile. In a room on the other side of the *cantorie* stands Donatello's extraordinary *Mary Magdalene*, while ranged around the walls are 16 statues removed from the Campanile. The museum's highlights, however, are the bronze panels crafted by Ghiberti for the Battistero doors – the focal point – paintings, mosaics and a glorious altarpiece (1459) by Antonio Pollaiuolo.

✚ 141 C5 ✉ Piazza del Duomo 9
☎ 055/230 2885 🕓 Apr–Oct Mon–Sat 9–7:30, Sun 9–1:40; Nov–Mar Mon–Sat 9–5:20, Sun 9–1:40. Closed 1 Jan, Easter Sun, 1 May, 15 Aug, 1 Nov, 8 Dec, 25–26 Dec
🖐 Expensive 🚌 1, 6, 7, 11, 14, 23

MUSEO DI SAN MARCO
Best places to see, pages 34–35.

MUSEO DI STORIA DELLA SCIENZA
Despite its fall from artistic grace after the Renaissance, Florence remained at the forefront of European science and learning, thanks to the work of men such as Galileo – born in nearby Pisa – and the enlightened patronage of rulers such as Ferdinand II and Cosimo II.

This well-presented and unexpectedly fascinating museum captures the essence of the times, each of the many rooms (over two floors) being devoted to a separate scientific theme or discipline.

The first floor opens with rooms devoted to counting machines and small instruments, including a case containing compasses that belonged to Michelangelo. Room 2's highlight is a beautifully enamelled quadrant; Room 3's is a lovely Tuscan astrolabe, two among hundreds of artefacts that display the Florentines' ability to turn even utilitarian objects into works of art. Room 4 features exhibits connected with Galileo, including the lens he used to discover the moons of Jupiter and – more bizarrely – some of the scientist's bones. Room 7, with its beautiful maps and globes, is one of the museum's loveliest corners.

The old microscopes of Room 9 lead to a salon devoted to the world's first scientific academy, the Accademia del Cimento, the body that – along with the Medici – was responsible for accumulating most of the museum's collection. Upstairs the museum delves into the mysteries of time and magnetism, followed by a sequence of less interesting pneumatic and hydrostatic displays. The best is saved until last: a roomful of alarming surgical instruments and horrifying anatomical waxworks.

✚ 141 E5 ✉ Piazza dei Giudici 1 ☎ 055/265 311 🕐 Oct–May Mon, Wed–Sat 9:30–5, Tue 9:30–1, 2nd Sun of month 10–1; Jun–Sep Mon, Wed–Fri 9:30–5, Tue, Sat 9:30–5 ✋ Expensive 🚌 23 ❓ Loan of excellent free guides to each floor available on request (in four languages, including English)

ORSANMICHELE

Orsanmichele is one of Florence's most intimate churches, providing a calm retreat from the crowds of Via dei Calzaiuoli. The earliest part of the site dates from 750, a small chapel situated in the kitchen garden *(orto)* of a Benedictine monastery. From these humble roots came its present name, which is a contraction of *San Michele ad Hortum* and *San Michele in Orto*. In 1280 the chapel was replaced with a grain market, a building destroyed by fire in 1304. In 1380 this was replaced with another church, the upper floor being retained as a granary.

Decoration of the new building was entrusted to the city's leading guilds, each of which was asked to commission a statue of its patron saint to adorn the exterior. After years of delays, statues were eventually secured from some of the greatest Renaissance artists, among them Verrocchio, Ghiberti, Donatello and Giambologna.

Some of these statues, such as Donatello's *St George*, have now been replaced with copies, the originals removed for safekeeping to the church museum and other city galleries. Others

occupy their original niches and have been cleaned as part of a large on-going restoration agenda. The interior, however, retains many of its oldest treasures, not least a magnificent glass and marble tabernacle (1348–59) by Andrea Orcagna, a work financed by votive offerings that flooded in after the Black Death of 1348. At its heart is a *Madonna and Child* (1347), a painting that is said to have inherited the miracle-working properties of a fresco on the site, destroyed in the fire of 1304. Most of the interior's frescoes, which were painted to complement the exterior sculptures, are depictions of the guild's patron saints.

✚ 141 D5 ✉ Orsanmichele: Via dei Calzaiuoli (main entrance to rear on Via dell'Arte della Lana). Museum: Via dell'Arte della Lana (opposite church entrance) ☎ 055/284 944 🕓 Tue–Fri 10–5, Sat–Sun 10–7:30. Museum closed for restoration 🎫 Free 🚌 In the pedestrian zone: nearest services 1, 6, 7, 11, 14, 23

PALAZZO MEDICI-RICCARDI

To the average bystander this palace looks like just one more grime-covered Florentine *palazzo*. Built for Cosimo de' Medici in 1444, it was designed by Michelozzo, the Medici's leading architect, and remained the family's main home until Cosimo I moved to the Palazzo Vecchio in 1540. Its heavily rusticated ground-floor exterior, almost fortress-like in appearance, was to influence many Florentine buildings in the century of palace-building that followed. Today much of the mansion is occupied by council offices, making the survival of one of the city's most charming fresco cycles all the more remarkable.

Benozzo Gozzoli painted the three-panel *Journey of the Magi* (1459) for Piero de' Medici, probably in tribute to the Compagnia dei Magi, one of the city's leading religious confraternities (of which the Medici were leading members). Tucked away in the tiny Cappella dei Magi, the cycle has been restored to stunning effect. The three principal panels deal with one of the three kings of the Nativity, though most interest derives from Gozzoli's inclusion of contemporary portraits among the sea of faces. On

the right wall, for example, the long procession is headed by a courtly figure probably intended to represent Lorenzo the Magnificent.

🕂 141 B5 ⊠ Via Cavour 3 ☎ 055/276 0340 or 276 0526 🕙 Thu–Tue 9–7 👋 Palace exterior and courtyard: free. Cappella dei Magi: moderate 🚌 1, 6, 7 ❓ Tickets can be reserved in advance by phone or at the ticket office

PALAZZO PITTI

Palaces and galleries do not come much larger than the Palazzo Pitti, home to the Medici for some 200 years and the setting for much of their private collection of paintings, silverware, costumes and miscellaneous objets d'art. The palace was begun in 1457 by Luca Pitti, a wealthy banker (possibly to a design by Brunelleschi), partly to upstage the Medici, then the implacable rivals of the Pittis. By 1549 the Pitti had fallen on hard times, forcing them – ironically – to sell to their old rivals. Once installed, the Medici altered the palace beyond recognition, adding two vast wings and countless additional rooms and salons.

These now house four separate museums, whose layout, ticketing and opening hours vary and can be slightly confusing. The main thing to see is the Galleria Palatina, home to a superlative collection of paintings (its entrance is to the rear right-hand side of the courtyard and up the stairs to the second floor). Within the Galleria, which is also something of a maze, you should start with the Sala di Venere, work down the following five state rooms, then return along the smaller parallel rooms to your starting point. The ceiling fresco in the Sala di Venere is the first of four, all by Piero da

Cortona, each depicting allegorical and mythological scenes inspired by the Medici. The room also contains the first of the gallery's many exceptional paintings, which here (as elsewhere) are wedged from floor to ceiling with little attempt at classification. Critics often complain at the arrangement and poor labelling, though this provides a vivid illustration of the collection's size and is how the Medici Grand Dukes chose to display their paintings.

The Sala di Apollo contains one of the gallery's many masterpieces, Titian's *Portrait of a Gentleman* (1540), along with the same artist's sensuous *Mary Magdalene* (1531) and Van Dyck's portraits of *Charles I and Henrietta Maria*. The next room, the Sala di Marte, features Rubens' huge *Consequences of War* (1638), an allegory of the Thirty Years' War. The next room, the Sala di Giove, was once the grand-ducal throne room. Today it is home to one of Raphael's finest portraits, the *Donna Velata*, (*Veiled Woman*, 1516). More Raphaels line the walls of the next two rooms, including the famous *Madonna della Seggiola* (1515), along with works by Andrea del Sarto, Tintoretto, Giorgione, Perugino, Velázquez and others. Highlights of the parallel rooms include Crisofano Allori's celebrated *Judith and Holofernes*, Caravaggio's *Sleeping Cupid* and a sublime *Madonna and Child* by Filippo Lippi.

The most worthwhile of the Pitti's other museums is the Museo degli Argenti, whose lavish salons display the silverware, *pietra dura* vases and other priceless (if often tasteless) objects accumulated by the Medici. The Galleria d'Arte Moderna contains some 30 rooms of Tuscan paintings (1784–1945), the most interesting of which are by the *Macchiaioli* group,

often called the Italian Impressionists. The Galleria del Costume has a sumptuous collection of clothes and costumes from the heyday of the Medici court. ✚ 140 F3 ✉ Piazza dei Pitti ☎ Galleria Palatina 055/238 8614. Museo degli Argenti 055/238 8709. Galleria d'Arte Moderna 056/238 8601. Galleria del Costume 055/238 8713 🕔 Galleria Palatina and Apartamenti Reali: Tue–Sun 8:15–6:50. Galleria del Costume, Museo degli Argenti and Museo delle Porcellane: hours as for Giardino di Boboli (➤ 56). Galleria d'Arte Moderna: Mon–Sat 8:15–6:50, Sun 8:15–1:50; closed 2nd, 4th Sun and 1st, 3rd, 5th Mon of month. Last ticket sold 45 mins before closing 🖐 Combined ticket for Galleria Palatina, Appartamenti Reali and Galleria d'Arte Moderna: expensive. Individual tickets for Galleria del Costume, Museo degli Argenti, Museo delle Porcellane: expensive. Combined ticket (except during major exhibitions) also includes Giardino di Boboli and Museo Barolini 🍴 Piazza dei Pitti (€) 🚌 36, 37, shuttle buses B and C ❓ Hours for the minor museums can change constantly according to the time of year, check with the tourist office

PALAZZO VECCHIO

The Palazzo Vecchio, designed by Arnolfo di Cambio, then also employed on the Duomo, was finished in 1303, but radically altered by Cosimo I in 1540 when he moved the Medici court here from the Palazzo Medici-Riccardi. When Cosimo moved again in 1550, this time to the 'new' Palazzo Pitti, the palace took its present name (vecchio means 'old').

Its courtyard (1453) was designed by Michelozzo, one of the Medici's preferred architects, and later adorned by Vasari with decorative panels. Vasari also built the staircase that leads to the palace's focal point, the vast but soulless Salone dei Cinquecento, built in 1495 to accommodate the 500 members of Florence's ruling assembly. Vasari decorated both its ceiling – whose gilt-laden paintings glorify Cosimo I – and the walls, whose six huge paintings (1563–5) depict a succession of Florentine military triumphs. Beneath them may be a series of unfinished frescoes

begun in 1506 by Michelangelo and Leonardo. A statue of *Victory* (1525) by Michelangelo stands almost opposite the Salone's entrance, while just off the chamber is the Studiolo (entrance door wall), a tiny but exquisitely decorated room. On the second floor enjoy the view from the Terrazza di Saturno, the many decorated rooms – notably Bronzino's Mannerist chapel – and the view of the Piazza della Signoria from the Sala d'Udienza. The Sala dei Gigli has frescoes by Domenico Ghirlandaio and Donatello's statue of *Judith and Holofernes*. Kids will enjoy the interactive workshops at the palace's innovative Museo dei Ragazzi (Children's Museum).

✚ 141 D5 ✉ Piazza della Signoria ☎ 055/276 8465 🕐 Mon–Wed, Fri–Sun 9–7, Thu 9–2; last admission 1 hour before closing. Closed Thu and 1 Jan, Easter Sun, 1 May, 15 Aug, 25–26 Dec 💷 Expensive (includes entry to Cappella Brancacci) 🚌 In the pedestrian zone: nearest services 19, 23, 31, 32 ❓ Hour-long tours (Mon–Sat; includes admission to palace) take visitors to parts of the palace normally closed: reserve in advance at ticket office

PIAZZA DELLA SIGNORIA

While the Piazza del Duomo was Florence's religious focus, the Piazza della Signoria has long served as the city's civic and political heart. Witness to countless momentous events across the centuries, such as the burning of Savonarola in 1498, it remains one of the city's busiest meeting places and the natural conclusion of the evening *passeggiata* (stroll) along Via dei Calzaiuoli. It was first enlarged in 1307 to accommodate the Palazzo dei Priori (now the Palazzo Vecchio), and was paved as early as 1385.

Sights include the Palazzo Vecchio; the Uffizi (off the square to the south); and the Loggia dei Lanzi, an outdoor gallery sheltering several outstanding pieces of sculpture. Greatest of these are Cellini's *Perseus* (1554) and Giambologna's contorted *Rape of the Sabine Women* (1583), though there are plans to replace these and other of the loggia's sculptures with copies.

More statues adorn the piazza itself. From left to right as you face the Palazzo Vecchio they include Giambologna's equestrian statue of Cosimo I (1587–94); the Neptune Fountain (1563–75) by Ammananti; next the *Marzocco*, a copy of Donatello's Florentine heraldic lion; *Judith and Holofernes* (1456–60), a copy of Donatello's statue in the Palazzo Vecchio; *David*, an 1873 copy of Michelangelo's most famous sculpture; and Bandinelli's *Hercules and Cacus* (1534), a work intended to symbolize Cosimo I, Florentine fortitude and the defeat of domestic enemies. On its unveiling the work was described by a fellow sculptor as a 'sack of melons'.

✚ 141 D5 ✉ Piazza della Signoria ☎ None ◷ Daily, 24 hours ✋ Free 🍴 Rivoire (Piazza della Signoria 5r; €€) 🚌 In the pedestrian zone: nearest services 19, 23, 31, 32

PONTE VECCHIO

The Ponte Vecchio and its huddle of old buildings are among the most familiar sights of Florence. Pitched close to the Arno's narrowest point, this is the last in a long succession of bridges on the site, dating back to Roman times. In 1944 it was the only Florentine bridge spared by the retreating Nazis, reputedly saved on Hitler's direct orders. In 1966 it was spared again – just – when it withstood the flood that brought death and destruction to much of Florence.

Until 1218 the bridge was the city's only river crossing, providing a vital lifeline between the old heart and the Oltrarno, on the Arno's southern bank. The present structure, which dates from 1345, was built to replace a bridge swept away in the floods of 1333 (some of the worst in the city's history). Its name ('Old Bridge') was coined

to distinguish it from the Arno's other bridge, the Ponte alla Carraia, originally built in 1218.

Shops first appeared on the bridge during the 14th century, most of them butchers and fishmongers. The next arrivals were the tanners, who soaked hides in the river before adding to the communal stench by tanning them with horse's urine. Across the top of the shops runs the Corridoio Vasariano, built by Vasari to enable Cosimo I to walk undisturbed between his home (the Palazzo Vecchio) and offices (the Uffizi). In 1593 Ferdinand I raised shop rents and decreed that only jewellers and goldsmiths should occupy the bridge. They remain to this day.

✚ 140 E4 ✉ Ponte Vecchio ☎ None ⏱ Daily, 24 hours ✋ Free
🚏 Pedestrianized ❓ Corridoio Vasariano occasionally open to visitors: consult Uffizi or tourist office for current opening times

SANTISSIMA ANNUNZIATA

The church of Santissima Annunziata lies on one of Florence's lesser-known but most architecturally pleasing squares. Laid out by Brunelleschi in the 1420s, the area was altered several times over the next 200 years, the most notable additions being an equestrian statue of Ferdinand I (1608) by Giambologna and two bizarre little fountains, the work of Giambologna's pupil, Pietro Tacca.

The church was built to praise the Annunciation, a crucial event in the life of the city: In the old Florentine calendar, the New Year began on the Feast of the Annunciation (25 March). It is now the mother church of the Servites, an order founded in 1234 by would-be servants (servi) of the Virgin.

The order built a chapel, which began drawing the crowds after 1252, when a painting begun by a Servite monk was miraculously completed by an angel. By 1450 so many pilgrims were coming that a new church, paid for by the Medici, was commissioned to house the painting. Via dei Servi was built at the same time to link

SS Annunziata and the Duomo, the two most important churches in the city dedicated to the Virgin.

The church's main sight is the inner courtyard, the Chiostro dei Voti (1447), swathed in frescoes by Andrea del Sarto, Jacopo Pontormo and Rosso Fiorentino. Inside the main body of the church lies Michelozzo's magnificent Tempietto (1448–61), built to shelter the miraculous painting. The first two chapels on the left feature celebrated works by Andrea del Castagno.

➕ 141 A6 ✉ Piazza della Santissima Annunziata ☎ 055/266 181 🕐 Daily 7:30–12:30, 4–6:30 🎟 Free 🚌 6, 31, 32 ❓ The eastern side of Piazza della SS Annunziata is dominated by a loggia (1493) built by Brunelleschi for the Ospedale degli Innocenti whose small Renaissance art collection and contrasting 'Men's' and 'Women's' cloisters are open to the public

Ospedale degli Innocenti

✉ Piazza della Santissima Annunziata 12 ☎ 055/249 1708 🕐 Mon–Sat 8:30–7, Sun 8:30–2. Closed 1 Jan, Easter Sun, 1 May, 15 Aug, 25–26 Dec 🎟 Moderate

SANT'APOLLONIA

Much of the former Benedictine convent of Sant'Apollonia has been converted into apartments, but the former refectory – the first Renaissance convent refectory in the city (1445) – features an entire wall frescoed with *The Last Supper* (1450), or *Cenacolo* in Italian, a subject that was often depicted in monastic and other religious eating places for obvious reasons. The work of Andrea del Castagno, it was uncovered in the 19th century, having been painted over by the nuns. It is an unsettling masterpiece, full of blood-red tones and featuring a devilish and black-bearded Judas.

➕ 141 A5 ✉ Via XXVII Aprile 1 ☎ 055 238 8607 🕐 Tue–Sat, 2nd, 4th Sun and 1st, 3rd, 5th Mon of month 8:15–1:50. Ticket office closes 30 mins earlier 🎟 Moderate 🚌 1, 6, 7, 10, 11 and other services to Piazza San Marco

SANTA CROCE

Best places to see, pages 38–39.

SAN LORENZO

San Lorenzo was founded in 393, making it one of the oldest churches in Florence. It served as the city's cathedral until the 7th century. A Romanesque church built on the site in 1060 survived until 1419, when Giovanni de' Medici and a group of parishioners offered to pay for a new church. Brunelleschi, then working on the Duomo, started work two years later, but progress faltered in the face of political and financial upheavals and only resumed when Giovanni's son, Cosimo de' Medici, offered 40,000 florins to ensure its completion (150 florins at this time could support a family for a year). As a result, the church became the Medici's dynastic church, while its rear portion, the Cappelle Medicee, became their private chapel (➤ 22–23).

The interior is an early Renaissance masterpiece. Brunelleschi created 'sails' of creamy wall interspersed with austere grey *pietra serena*. Artistic highlights include Rosso Fiorentino's *Marriage of the Virgin* (second altar on the right) and Desiderio da Settignano's *Pala del Sacramento* (1451–68), on the wall at the end of the right nave.

In the middle of the church stand two raised pulpits (1455–66), among the last works of Donatello (and pupils), and in front of the high altar brass grilles mark the tomb of Cosimo de' Medici (with a plaque inscribed *Pater Patriae* – Father of the Fatherland). The *Martyrdom of St. Laurence* (1565–9), left of the two pulpits, is a graphic painting by Bronzino. In a chapel around the corner is a cenotaph (monument) to Donatello, who died in 1464 and was buried near Cosimo, his friend and patron. Brunelleschi's Sagrestia Vecchia, or Old Sacristy (1421), a simple architectural gem, is entered from the left transept of the church. On the left as you enter stands the bronze and porphyry tomb of Giovanni and Piero de' Medici (Cosimo de' Medici's sons), and in the middle is the tomb of Giovanni and Piccarda, Cosimo's parents and founders of the Medici fortune.

Most of the sacristy's decoration (1434–43) is by Donatello, most notably the eight tondi showing the Evangelists and scenes from the life of St John (Giovanni's patron saint). The reliefs above the doors of the end wall portray Cosmos and Damian, the Medici's patron saints, and saints Laurence and Stephen, protectors of Florence.

From the church cloisters, stairs lead to the Biblioteca Laurenziana, begun in 1524 to house the Medici's vast 100-year old library, collected by agents sent as far afield as Germany and the Middle East. Michelangelo designed the Ricetto (Vestibule), with its revolutionary use of space, and almost every detail of the

library Reading Room – even the desks. The four rooms beyond contain a fraction of the books and manuscripts.

🚇 140 B4 ✉ Piazza San Lorenzo ☎ San Lorenzo: 055/216 634. Biblioteca Laurenziana: 055/214 443 or 210 760 🕓 San Lorenzo: Mon–Sat 10–5. Biblioteca Laurenziana: Mon–Sat 8:30–1:30 👆 Inexpensive 🚉 In the pedestrian zone

SANTA MARIA NOVELLA

Santa Maria Novella ranks second only to Santa Croce in the pantheon of great Florentine churches. Begun as a simple chapel in the 9th century, it was rebuilt in 1094 and christened Santa Maria delle Vigne (Mary of the Vineyards). It then passed to the Dominicans, who in 1246 began a new church. The Romanesque façade was not finished until 1456, when Leon Battista Alberti completed the multi-hued frontage.

The lofty Gothic interior has several important frescoes, the most famous of which is Masaccio's *Trinità* (1428), midway down the left wall, one of the first Renaissance paintings to put the new theories of perspective to good use. Close by is Brunelleschi's pulpit (1443–52), where the Inquisition first denounced Galileo for agreeing with Copernicus that the earth revolved around the sun, and not vice versa.

Many of the church's chapels were commissioned by leading Renaissance businessmen. Banker Filippo Strozzi employed Filippino Lippi to fresco the Cappella di Filippo Strozzi with scenes from the life of his namesake, St Philip (Filippo) the Apostle. The chapel to its right, the Cappella Bardi, features faded 14th-century frescoes, some attributed to Cimabue, Giotto's first teacher.

To the left of the Strozzi chapel, in the chancel, is Domenico Ghirlandaio's beautiful fresco cycle on the *Life of the Virgin* (left wall) and *Life of St John the Baptist* (right wall). Despite their religious themes, these are actually vignettes of daily life in 15th-century Florence; they were commissioned by another banker, Giovanni Tornabuoni, whose relations appear in several scenes.

More frescoes (1351–7), the work of Nardo di Cione, adorn the Cappella Strozzi (up steps at the top left-hand side of the church): *Paradiso* (left wall); the *Last Judgement* (behind the altar) and a map-like *Inferno* (right wall). The altarpiece is by Nardo's brother, Andrea di Cione, better known as Orcagna, and shows *Christ Giving the Keys to St Peter and the Book of Knowledge to Thomas Aquinas* (the chapel is dedicated to Aquinas).

Left of Santa Maria's façade is the entrance to the church museum and Chiostro Verde (Green Cloister), named after the green pigment of its badly faded frescoes. Despite the

deterioration, many of the panels are superb – especially Paolo Uccello's *Universal Deluge* (1430), whose lurching composition illustrates his obsession with perspective. Notice the arks to either side of the picture, depicted before and after the Flood.

Off the cloister lies the Cappellone degli Spagnuoli, once used by the Spanish entourage of Eleanor of Toledo, wife of Cosimo I. It features one of the city's most striking fresco cycles, the work of Andrea da Firenze.

The left wall shows *The Triumph of Doctrine,* with Thomas Aquinas enthroned amid the Virtues and Doctors of the Church.

The right wall portrays *The Work and Triumph of the Dominican Order*, with St Dominic unleashing the 'hounds of the Lord' (*Domini canes,* a pun on 'Dominicans'). The four women are the Four Vices, surrounded by dancing and other debaucheries. A nearby friar hears confessions before sending the saved heavenwards; above the kneeling pilgrims are portraits of Dante, Petrarch, Giotto and others.

✠ 140 B3 ✉ Piazza Santa Maria Novella ☎ Church: 055/215 918. Museum: 055/282 187 🕓 Santa Maria Novella: Mon–Thu 9–5, Fri 1–5, Sat 9–5, Sun 1–5. Museo di Santa Maria Novella: Mon–Thu, Sat 9–5. Closed Fri and 1 Jan, Easter Sun, 25 Apr, 1 May, 15 Aug, 25–26 Dec ✋ Santa Maria Novella: free. Museo di Santa Maria Novella: inexpensive 🍴 In Piazza Santa Maria Novella (€) 🚌 All services to the rail station ❓ Guided tours of the church occasionally available

SAN MINIATO AL MONTE

The most beautiful church in Florence takes its name from St Minias, a Greek or Armenian Christian merchant who was martyred in Florence in AD250. According to legend the saint picked up his severed head and carried it from his place of execution (close to Piazza della Signoria) across the Arno to the hilltop site where his church now stands. Most of the present building dates from 1013, making it among the city's oldest churches.

The Romanesque façade (1090–1270) features a mosaic of Christ, Mary and St Minias (1260) and a gilded eagle clasping a bale of wool – symbol of the Arte di Calimala, the wealthy guild that was made responsible for the church's fabric in 1228.

The breathtaking interior is dominated by a sumptuous painted wooden ceiling (1322) and a famous inlaid floor (1207), reputedly inspired by Sicilian fabrics, and patterned with lions, doves and the signs of the zodiac. The capitals on the pillars of the nave are Roman and Byzantine originals. In the left-hand aisle is the Cappella del Cardinale del Portogallo, a Renaissance masterpiece complete with paintings, glazed terracotta and funerary sculpture, the works of sculptor Antonio Rossellino and painters Baldovinetti and two brothers Antonio and Pietro Pollaiuolo. The Cardinal of

Portugal, whose uncle was King of Portugal, died in Florence in 1459 and was buried here. At the end of the nave, alongside Michelozzo's free-standing Cappella del Crocifisso (1448), steps lead to the raised choir and a magnificent carved pulpit and screen (1207). The sacristy, off to the right boasts a vivid fresco cycle by Spinello Aretino depicting Scenes from the Life of St Benedict (1387).

✚ 141 F6 (off map) ✉ Off Viale Galileo Galilei ☎ 055/234 2731 ⊙ Summer daily 8–7:30; winter Mon–Sat 8–12, 3–6, Sun 3–6 ✋ Free 🍽 In Viale Galileo Galilei (€–€€) 🚌 12, 13

SANTA TRINITÀ

Santa Trinità is something of an architectural curiosity. Its flamboyant baroque exterior makes a striking contrast with the

calm, Gothic assurance of its interior. Founded in 1092, it was rebuilt between 1258 and 1280 – possibly to a design by Nicola Pisano – and the façade was added by Buontalenti in 1593.

The dusky, atmospheric interior has several wonderful works of art, most notably Domenico Ghirlandaio's frescoes (1483) in the Cappella Sassetti (the right-hand chapel to the right of the high altar). They represent

episodes from the life of St Francis and were commissioned by
Francesco Sassetti in a bid to outdo his rival, Francesco Tornabuoni,
who had paid for the frescoes in Santa Maria Novella, also by
Ghirlandaio.

The panel portraying *St Francis Receiving the Rule* in the
lunette above the altar is famous for its setting – the Piazza della
Signoria – and its portraits, which include Sassetti, who worked
for the Medici bank, between his son, Federigo, and Lorenzo the
Magnificent. On the stairs stand the humanist Poliziano and three
of his pupils, the sons of Lorenzo the Magnificent.

The chapel's altarpiece, also by Ghirlandaio (1485), depicts *The
Adoration of the Magi*, combining classical and Christian motifs
(notice the Roman sarcophagus). Sassetti and his wife are
portrayed to either side. Other works of art include Lorenzo
Monaco's early 15th-century frescoes (fourth chapel on the right),
the *Tomb of Bishop Federighi* (1454–7) by Luca della Robbia
(second chapel left of the altar) and frescoes by Neri di Bicci and
Bicci di Lorenzo (fourth chapel on the left).

✝ 140 D3 ✉ Piazza di Santa Trinità ☎ 055/216 912 🕐 Mon–Sat 8–12,
4–6, Sun 4–6. Summer hours may be longer 👆 Free 🚌 6, 11, 31, 32, 36, 37

Northern Tuscany

Northern Tuscany is a region of secret corners and little-known towns, a rich and fascinating area often ignored by visitors anxious to explore the more celebrated sights south of Florence.

In Lucca, it has one of the loveliest towns in Italy, a beautiful medley of quiet streets, Romanesque churches, quaint squares and imposing city walls. Nearby Pisa is less charming, but the sights of the Campo dei Miracoli – the famous Leaning Tower, Duomo and Baptistery – make up one of Europe's finest architectural ensembles.

Smaller towns such as Pistoia and Carrara also have their artistic treasures, while Viareggio is a busy but appealing resort if you want a day by the sea. Carrara is also known for its marble, quarried for centuries from the Alpi Apuane. These spectacular mountains form part of the Garfagnana, a varied region of dulcet valleys, wild uplands, lonely lakes and beguiling rural villages.

Pisa

ALPI APUANE

The Apuan Alps contain Tuscany's most spectacular scenery, forming a jagged crest of mountains above the Versilian coast north of Pisa and Lucca. Marble mines streak their western flanks, the source for centuries of stone that has served sculptors from Michelangelo to Henry Moore. On their eastern borders, chestnut-covered slopes fall away to the Garfagnana, a dulcet valley by the pleasant little towns of Barga and Castelnuovo (Barga, in particular, is well worth visiting for its lovely cathedral). Well-marked trails criss-cross the slopes, wending through woods or cresting the panoramic and craggy summit ridges. Excellent walking maps of the region are widely available, making it easy to undertake light strolls or proper hikes. Stazzema and Levigliani make good departure points in the west; late May is the best time to see the area's renowned spring flowers. Driving is also a delight, the excellent folk museum in San Pellegrino in Alpe (16km/10 miles northeast of Castelnuovo) being a particularly good target. The mountains have protected park status, and are earmarked for future national park designation.

🗺 132 C3–D4 🚆 Pisa to Pietrasanta or Massa; Lucca to Castelnuovo di Garfagnana 🛈 Piazzale Giuseppe Verdi ☎ 0583/442 944 or 0583/583 150

BARGA

Barga is the most interesting village in the Garfagnana, perched high on the slopes of the Orecchiella mountains and looking across the valley to the jagged peaks of the Alpi Apuane. A lovely setting aside, its main attraction is the honey-stoned Duomo, San

Cristofano, founded in the ninth century at the village's highest point, its terrace offering a glorious view over the rooftops to the mountains beyond. Behind a lovely Romanesque facade, the interior contains a sublime pulpit, probably the work of a 13th-centurty sculptor from Como in northern Italy. Also noteworthy is a large 10th- or 12th-century wooden sculpture of St Christopher. Elsewhere, be sure to visit Santissimo Crocifisso dei Bianchi (irregular hours), an extravagantly decorated baroque chapel just below the Duomo, and the **Museo Civico del Territorio di Barga,** a modest but interesting museum devoted to the region's geological and archaeological history.

✚ 133 D5 🚃 From Lucca to Barga station, 3.5km (2 miles) from the village
ℹ️ Via di Mezzo 45 ☎ 0583 724 743; www.barganews.com

Museo Civico del Territorio di Barga

✉️ Palazzo Pretorio, Arringo del Duomo ☎ 0583 711 100 🕐 Hours vary: call for latest details ✋ Moderate

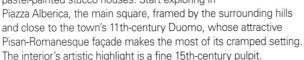

CARRARA

The mountains around Carrara have been quarried for their grey-white marble for centuries, and today, with over 200 mines and around 700,000 tonnes of stone extracted a year, the region is the world's largest marble producer. While the mines may blight the surroundings, the centre of hilltop Carrara itself is delightful, full of medieval streets and pretty, pastel-painted stucco houses. Start exploring in Piazza Alberica, the main square, framed by the surrounding hills and close to the town's 11th-century Duomo, whose attractive Pisan-Romanesque façade makes the most of its cramped setting. The interior's artistic highlight is a fine 15th-century pulpit.

Then, either drive or a take a local bus towards Marina di Carrara, to visit the **Museo Civico di Marmo,** an impressive museum that delves into the history and production of the marble. You should also try to venture into the hills immediately around the town to visit some of the working marble mines. The most accessible are signposted off the road to Colonnata, 8km (5 miles) from the town: look for signs saying *Visita Cave* or *Cava di Marmo*. Larger mines can be visited farther south around Monte Corchia.

✠ 132 D3

Museo Civico di Marmo

✉ Via XX Settembre, 2km (1.2 miles) southwest of town centre 🕐 Jul–Aug daily 10–8; May, Jun, Sep daily 10–6; Oct–Apr Mon–Sat 9–5 💷 Moderate

EMPOLI

Empoli is a predominantly modern, industrial town and rail junction, a place unseen by most visitors, the majority of whom pass through on the train en route for Florence, Pisa or Siena. If you do have an hour to spare, make first for the central Piazza Farinata degli Uberti, named after the leader of the Sienese army that defeated the Florentines at the Battle of Montaperti in 1260. The square's principal historic building is the Collegiata, founded as early as the fifth century, with a venerable, Romanesque lower portion and an upper section that was restored after damage in the Second World War.

Next to the Collegiata is the **Museo della Collegiata,** home to an impressive collection of paintings and sculptures, including triptychs by Lorenzo di Monaco, a rare Pietà by Masolino, Lorenzo di Bicci's *St Nicholas of Tolentino Saving Empoli from the Plague* (note the background view of medieval Empoli as it appeared in the 1440s) and sculptures by Tuscan masters Mino da Fiesole and Bernardo Rossellino.

Empoli was the birthplace of the composer and pianist Ferruccio Busoni (1866–1924) and commemorates its most famous son with a series of recitals from October to May.

www.comune.empoli.fi.it

✚ 133 F7

Museo della Collegiata

✉ Piazzetta della Propositora 🕐 Tue–Sun 9–12, 4–7 ✋ Inexpensive

GARFAGNANA

The Garfagana is one of Tuscany's least-visited scenic enclaves, a wonderfully varied region north of Lucca that consists of verdant valleys, pastoral meadows, thick forests, the spectacular peaks of the Alpi Apuane to the west and the more dulcet uplands of the Orecchiella to the east. The region centres on the valley of the Serchio, which carries the area's main road and rail link, as well as the rather lacklustre main town, Castelnuovo di Garfagnana.

You'll need a car to get the most out of the region, especially if you want to visit the best of its upland villages (notably Barga) or explore the many dramatic and scenic small roads that wind into the mountains. One of the best roads runs through the hamlet of San Pellegrino in Alpe, 16km (10 miles) east of Castelnuovo, where there is a superb museum of rural life, the **Museo Etnografico Provinciale.**

The same roads can also be used to reach high-level trailheads for some excellent hiking. Both the Alpi Apuane and Orecchiella are protected areas, and have numerous marked trails. Good walking maps are widely available locally. You may also want to visit Tuscany's most spectacular cave system, the **Grotta del Vento,** in Fornovo, 9km (5.5 miles) west of Barga's railway station. Note, however, that it can be busy and is rather commercialized.

🚩 133 C5

🛈 Piazza delle Erbe, Castelnuovo di Garfagnana ☎ 0583 65 169

Museo Ethnografico Provinciale

✉ Via del Voltone 14 ☎ 0583 649 072 ✋ Inexpensive

Grotta del Vento

✉ Fornovo Lasso 🕐 Apr–Oct 1-, 2-, 3-hour tours on the hour 10–6; Nov–Mar 1-hour tours Mon–Sat 10–5, Sun 1-, 2-, 3-hour tours

LUCCA

Lucca is one of Tuscany's gems, filled with cobbled streets, tiny
Romanesque churches, bristling towers and lovely medieval
buildings. The town began life as a Roman colony, later becoming
Tuscany's first Christian town and the seat of the region's Imperial
rulers (the Margraves). Its medieval wealth was second only to
Florence, thanks to its banking and textiles, allowing it to dominate
western Tuscany for centuries. Independent until 1799, it passed to
Napoleon in 1809 (the town was ruled by his sister, Elisa Baciocchi)
and then to the Grand Duchy of Tuscany in 1847.

Walking Lucca's streets is a pleasure in itself, but no trip to the
city would be complete without wandering part of the city walls,
4km (2.5 miles) in all, built in the 16th and 17th centuries as a
defence against the Tuscan dukes. From their tree-lined ramparts
you can enjoy panoramas over the pantiled rooftops, occasionally
descending to explore sights such as the peaceful little **Giardino
Botanico** (Botanic Gardens), in the city's southeast corner.

www.comune.lucca.it

✚ 133 E5

🛈 Piazzale Giuseppe Verdi ☎ 0583/442 944 ⏰ Daily 9–7 (6pm Nov–Mar)

Giardino Botanico

✉ Via dell'Orto Botanico 14 ☎ 0583/442 160 ⏰ Jul to mid-Sep Mon–Sat 10–7; May–Jun 10–6; Jul to mid-Sep 10–7; Apr, mid-Sep to mid-Oct 10–5; mid-Oct to Mar Mon–Fri 9:30–12:30, by appointment only 🖐 Inexpensive

Duomo di San Martino

Lucca's stunning Romanesque cathedral is one of Tuscany's architectural masterpieces. The asymmetrical façade, begun in 1070, is famous for its carved reliefs, especially those over the central door – the *Life of St Martin* and *Labours of the Months* – and those of the left portal (1233), probably by Nicola Pisano. Matteo Civitali (1435–1501), a local sculptor, took charge inside, where he was responsible for the inlaid floor, pulpit, water stoups, two tombs in the south transept and the vast *Tempietto* (midway down the nave), an octagonal structure built to house the *Volto Santo*, a 'true effigy' of Christ carved after the Crucifixion (probably a 13th-century fake). This statue, which is robed rather than naked, in the Byzantine style, is carried through the streets of Lucca on the eve of the Feast of the Holy Cross (13 September). The interior's highlight is Jacopo della Quercia's *Tomb of Illaria del Carretto* (1410), one of Italy's most beautiful tombs (it is currently housed off the right nave: there is a small admission charge to view it). The cathedral also contains paintings by Fra Bartolomeo, Bronzino, Tintoretto and Domenico Ghirlandaio. The nearby **Museo della Cattedrale** has a collection of religious and other objects.

Duomo

✉ Piazza San Martino ⏰ Apr–Oct daily 7–7; Nov–Mar daily 7–5

Museo della Cattedrale

✉ Piazza Antelminelli ☎ 0583/490 530 ⏰ Apr–Oct daily 10–6; Nov–Mar Mon–Sat 10–2, Sun 10–5 🖐 Moderate. Joint ticket with Church of San Giovanni and Museo della Cathedrale

Museo Nazionale di Villa Guinigi

The Museo Nazionale di Villa Guinigi, at the eastern end of
the town, has a major collection of sculpture; paintings; and
archaeological fragments, including objects dating back to the
Etruscan and Roman periods. Among the exhibits are works by
Jacopo della Quercia, Matteo Civitali, Fra Bartolomeo and paintings
by anonymous Sienese and Lucchese masters. More paintings
can be seen across the city in the **Pinacoteca Nazionale,** housed
in the Palazzo Mansi, a wonderful rococo palace.

✉ Via della Quarquonia ☎ 0583/496 033 🕓 Tue–Sat 8:30–7:30, Sun
8:30–1:30 🎫 Moderate or expensive with joint ticket with Pinacoteca
Nazionale di Palazzo Mansi

Pinacoteca Nazionale di Palazzo Mansi

✉ Via Galli Tassi 43 ☎ 0583/55 570 or 0583/ 583 461 🕓 Tue–Sat 8:30–7,
Sun and public hols 8:30–1 🎫 Moderate or expensisve joint ticket
with Villa Guinigi

San Frediano

San Frediano (1112–47), the third of Lucca's major churches,
is dominated by a superb 13th-century façade mosaic,
while the dark interior features a wealth of sculptures and
paintings. One of the main attractions is the magnificent
Fonta Lustrale, a large and intricately carved 12th-century
font. Behind it, a carved *Annunciation* by Andrea della
Robbia is framed by festoons of terracotta fruit. Close by is the
tomb of St Zita, patron saint of serving maids. The Cappella Trenta
(fourth chapel on the left) features two floor tombs and a sculpted
altarpiece (1422) by Jacopo della Quercia; the second chapel in the
same aisle contains the city's best fresco cycle: Amico Aspertini's
16th-century scenes from the lives of San Frediano and St
Augustine as well as the *Arrival of the Volto Santo in Lucca* (see
above). Just to the southeast of the church is Piazza Anfiteatro, an
evocative square whose oval of crumbling houses mirrors the
shape of the Roman amphitheatre that stood here until the 12th

century. Many were partly built with stone from the amphitheatre.

A short distance south of Piazza Anfiteatro (walk via San Pietro Somaldi for its lovely façade) brings you to the **Torre Guinigi,** an eccentric city landmark built as a defensive tower by the Guinigi, one of Lucca's leading medieval families. A grove of ilex trees sprouts from its summit, and it has lovely views over the city.

✉ Piazza San Frediano ☎ None 🕐 Mon–Sat 8:30–12, 3–5, Sun 10:30–5 (except during services) 💵 Free

Torre Guinigi

✉ Via Sant'Andrea 41 ☎ 0583/48 524 🕐 May–Aug daily 9am–11pm; Apr, Sep, Oct 9–9; Mar 9–7:30; Feb 9:30–6; Nov–Dec 10–6; Jan 10–5. Closed 25 Dec 💵 Moderate

San Michele in Foro

Lucca's streets focus on Piazza San Michele, site of the old Roman forum *(foro)*, and now home to San Michele, one of Italy's loveliest churches. Some 300 years in the making, its façade is a wonderful confection of pillars, arcades and tiny twisted columns. The interior, by contrast, is plain, apart from a della Robbia terracotta and Filippino Lippi's *Saints Jerome, Sebastian, Roch and Helena.* West of the square lies the **Casa Natale di Puccini,** birthplace of Giacomo Puccini (1858–1924). There is a monument to Lucca's war dead just off Piazza Napoleone.

✉ Piazza San Michele ☎ None 🕐 Daily 7:40–12, 3–6. Closed 1 Jan, 25 Dec 💵 Free

MONTECATINI TERME

Montecatini Terme is one of Italy's most popular and exclusive spa towns. The nine natural sulphur springs, each with its own building, are found in the Parco delle Terme, dominated by the Terme Leopoldine. Even if you are not taking a full cure in one of the town's many hotels, you can sample the waters in the spa café. There is little to see in the town, but it is fun to ride the funicular (Apr–Oct only) to Montecatini Alto, the town's original medieval heart, where Piazza Giusti offers some fine views.

➕ 133 E6 ℹ Viale Verdi 66 ☎ 0572 772 244; www.termemontecatini.it

PISA

Pisa has more to offer than its famous leaning tower (➤ 40–41), not least the ensemble of sights on Piazza dei Miracoli, the broad grassy square that encloses not only the tower but also the town's cathedral, Baptistery and Camposanto. Begun in 1152, the **Baptistery** (Italy's largest) is a mixture of Romanesque and Gothic, the latter added by Nicola and Giovanni Pisano between 1270 and 1290. Nicola also carved the exceptional pulpit; the interior is otherwise bare, except for an octagonal font by Guido da Como.

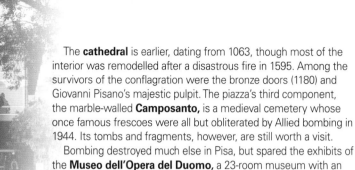

The **cathedral** is earlier, dating from 1063, though most of the interior was remodelled after a disastrous fire in 1595. Among the survivors of the conflagration were the bronze doors (1180) and Giovanni Pisano's majestic pulpit. The piazza's third component, the marble-walled **Camposanto,** is a medieval cemetery whose once famous frescoes were all but obliterated by Allied bombing in 1944. Its tombs and fragments, however, are still worth a visit.

Bombing destroyed much else in Pisa, but spared the exhibits of the **Museo dell'Opera del Duomo,** a 23-room museum with an uneven collection of paintings, sculptures and other objects. The **Museo Nazionale di San Matteo,** Pisa's main civic museum, is similarly hit-and-miss, but includes works by Masaccio, Donatello and Simone Martini. The town's loveliest church is Santa Maria della Spina, named after a spine *(spina)* from Christ's Crown of Thorns kept inside.

www.pisa.turismo.toscana.it

✚ 132 F4

ℹ Piazza della Stazione 11 and Piazza del Duomo ☎ 050/560 464, 542 291, 541 800 or 542 344

Duomo, Baptistery, Camposanto and Museo dell'Opera

✉ Campo (Piazza) dei Miracoli ☎ 050/560 547 (all sights) 🕒 Duomo: late Mar–Sep Mon–Sat 10–8, Sun 1–8; Mar, Oct Mon–Sat 10–7, Sun 1–7; Nov–Feb Mon–Sat 10–1, 2–5, Sun 2–5. Baptistery, Camposanto, Museo dell'Opera: end Mar–Oct daily 8–8; first 2 weeks Mar daily 10–6; 3rd week Mar daily 10–7; Oct daily 9–7; Nov–Feb daily 10–5 (25 Dec–7 Jan 9–6) 🖐 Moderate (all sights); also a variety of combined tickets to a different sights

Museo Nazionale di San Matteo

✉ Lungarno Mediceo ☎ 050/541 865 🕒 Tue–Sat 8:30–7, Sun 8:30–1 🖐 Moderate

PISTOIA

Pistoia's industrial outskirts deter most visitors, which is a shame, for the town boasts a medieval centre and a group of churches and monuments that stand comparison with any in Tuscany. Piazza del Duomo, its captivating main square, is home to the Campanile, a former Lombard watchtower; several medieval palaces; a 14th-century baptistery; and the arched façade of the town's **cathedral.**

The last contains a font by Benedetto da Maiano (entrance wall) and the tomb of Cino da Pistoia (1337), writer and friend of Dante. The chief highlight is the St James Altar (1287–1456), Italy's finest piece of medieval silverware. The work contains some 628 figures and depicts episodes from the Old and New Testaments. To the left and rear of the cathedral is the **Museo Civico,** with a collection of paintings and sculptures.

Elsewhere in the town be sure to see the 12th-century church of San Bartolomeo in Pantano, which has a pulpit (1250) by Guido da Como; San Giovanni Fuorcivitas, known for its pulpit by Guglielmo da Pisa (1270); and Sant'Andrea, also famous for its pulpit (1301), an outstanding work by Giovanni Pisano. Sculpture of a different kind adorns the façade of the Ospedale del Ceppo, a 13th-century hospital decorated with a colourful glazed terracotta frieze (1514–25) by Giovanni della Robbia *(The Seven Works of Mercy)*. Finally, visit the Cappella del Tau, a deconsecrated church noted for its 14th-century Gothic frescoes.

www.comune.pistoia.it

➕ 133 D7

🛈 Palazzo dei Vescovi, Piazza del Duomo 4 ☎ 0573/21 622

Cathedral

✉ Piazza del Duomo ☎ 0573/25 095 🕓 Daily 8–12:30, 4–7 💷 Cathedral: free. St James Altar: inexpensive

Museo Civico

✉ Palazzo del Comune, Piazza del Duomo ☎ 0573/3711 or 0573/371 214 🕓 Apr–Oct Tue–Sat 10–6, Sun 9:30–12:30; Nov–Feb Tue–Sat 10–5, Sun 9:30–12:30 💷 Inexpensive

PRATO

Prato is Tuscany's largest city after Florence, its wealth founded on a centuries-old textile industry, which still continues. It receives few visitors, yet beyond its modern suburbs is a perfectly preserved historic heart, bounded by old walls and filled with artistic and architectural treasures, galleries and museums. The main sights are the **Castello dell'Imperatore,** begun around 1230 for Emperor Frederick II, the Renaissance

church of Santa Maria delle Carceri, and the Duomo, known for its **museum,** Filippo Lippi's frescoes (1452–66) around the high altar, a fresco cycle (1392–5) by Agnolo Gaddi and a magnificent pulpit by Michelozzo and Donatello.

➕ 133 E8

Museo dell'Opera del Duomo

✉ Piazza del Duomo 49 ☎ 0574 29339 🕓 Mon, Wed–Sat 9:30–12:30, 3–6:30; Sun 9:30–12:30. Closed Tue 💷 Moderate

Castello dell'Imperatore

✉ Viale Piave ☎ 0574 38207 🕓 Apr–Sep Mon, Wed–Sat 9–1, 4–7; Oct–Mar Mon, Wed–Sun 9–1. Closed Tue 💷 Inexpensive. Moderate for combined ticket with Museo dell'Opera

VIAREGGIO

Tuscany's main seaside resort is just an hour or so by train from
Florence, and in summer it is often full of Florentines escaping
the city's bustle. This can make it busy, but rarely unpleasant, for
the resort has a distinctly elegant air, thanks to long avenues of
palms, numerous large stucco-fronted hotels, an airy waterfront
promenade, and a handful of Liberty-style frontages. Most of the
last are at the eastern end of Viale Regina Margherita, the town's
long waterfront boulevard, clustered around the Gran Caffè
Margherita, an historic café. The beaches are well groomed, but
note that most are private concessions *(stabilimenti)*, where an
entry fee of a few euros buys you the rental of towels and a sun-
lounger plus bar, restaurant and bathroom facilities.
www.versilia.turismo.toscana.it

✚ 132 E4

ℹ Viale Carducci 10 ☎ 0584 962 233. There is also a seasonal information
kiosk (Apr–Sep) at the railway station ☎ 0584 46 382

Southern Tuscany

Mention Tuscany, and Southern Tuscany is the region that readily comes to mind, filled with the classic landscapes of olive groves, vineyards, cypress-topped hills and poppy-filled fields, and scattered with elegant villas, pretty farmhouses and countless sun-hazed hill towns.

Siena

At its heart is Siena, the finest medieval town in Europe, centred on the Campo, its majestic square, best known as the stage for the twice-yearly Palio horse race. Elsewhere, virtually every town has something of interest – Arezzo, Cortona, Montalcino, Pienza, San Gimignano, Volterra – as do the region's many pockets of glorious countryside, notably the wooded hills of Chianti and the pastoral heartlands south of Siena, each graced with pretty villages, sweeping views and beautiful, ancient abbeys such as Sant'Antimo and Monte Oliveto Maggiore.

ABBADIA DI MONTE OLIVETO MAGGIORE

Tuscany's finest working monastery was founded in the 14th century by the Olivetans, an offshoot of the Benedictines, and is set in glorious countryside, with sweeping views. Much of the large abbey complex remains closed to visitors, but you are able to see the Chiostro Grande, or Grand Cloister, among other things, which is home to a majestic fresco cycle on the *Life of St Benedict*, painted between 1497 and 1508 by Luca Signorelli and Antonio Bazzi, better known as Il Sodoma. The cycle's many panels are ranged around the walls of the cloister, and contain a wealth of wonderful narrative detail. Also be sure to see the finely carved choir stalls (1500–20) in the baroque abbey church.

✚ 138 D4 ✉ Monte Oliveto Maggiore, Chiusure, near Buonconvento
☎ 0577 707 652 🕐 Daily 9:15–12, 3:15–5:45 (5 in winter) 🖐 Free

AREZZO

This largely modern town merits a visit if only for Piero della Francesca's *The Legend of the True Cross* (1452–66), one of Italy's most famous fresco cycles. Ranged across the chancel of **San Francesco,** a church at the heart of the old town, the cycle describes how the tree from which Eve plucked the forbidden fruit becomes the cross of Christ's crucifixion. Although damaged in places, the frescoes have been restored, emphasizing the calm tones and subtlety for which Piero is renowned.

The Piazza Grande, the town's precipitously sloping main square, is graced by the Loggia di Vasari (1573) and Palazzetto della Fraternità della Laici, built for a lay confraternity and distinguished by a beautiful doorway and lunette tabernacle (1434) by Bernardino Rossellino. To its left protrudes the arcaded apse of Santa Maria, a Romanesque church whose façade overlooks the Corso Italia. The interior has a superb altarpiece (1320) by Pietro Lorenzetti.

To the north stands the **Duomo,** whose airy Gothic interior is known for Piero della Francesca's fresco of *Mary Magdalene* and 14th-century *Tomb of Bishop Guido Tarlati* (end of the north aisle). Also worth a look are the cathedral museum, filled with paintings, sculpture and terracotta; the nearby **Casa Vasari,** birthplace of the 16th-century painter and writer; and the **Museo d'Arte Medievale e Moderna,** with an eclectic assortment of paintings and objects, including five rooms of ceramics and paintings by the *Macchiaioli*, the so-called 'Italian Impressionists'.

www.apt.arezzo.it

✚ 139 B6

🛈 Piazza della Repubblica 28 ☎ 0575/377 678

San Francesco

✉ Piazza San Francesco ☎ 0575/302 001 or 0575/352 727; www.ticketeria.it 🕓 Mon–Fri 9–7, Sat 9–6, Sun 1–6. Closes earlier in winter. Prebooked guided tours every 30 mins 🖐 Moderate. Tickets must be prebooked by phone or (off-season) in person an hour before visit

Duomo

✉ Piazza del Duomo ☎ 0575/23 991 🕓 Daily 7/8:30–12:30, 3–6:30/7 🖐 Free

Casa Vasari

✉ Via XX Settembre 55 ☎ 0575/40901 🕓 Mon, Wed–Sat 9–7, Sun 9–1 🖐 Free

Museo d'Arte Medievale e Moderna

✉ Via di San Lorentino 8 ☎ 0575/409050 🕓 Tue–Sun 9–7. Closed Mon and 1 Jan, 1 May, 25 Dec 🖐 Moderate

CORTONA

Etruscan Cortona is a beguiling little hill town, with ancient walls ringed with olives and vineyards. A short walk from Piazza della Repubblica, which forms the

heart of the old town, leads to the **Museo Diocesano,** noted for a handful of Renaissance paintings. The best-known are the glorious *Annunciation* (1428–30) and *Madonna Enthroned with Saints*, both by Fra Angelico.

The town's other major gallery is the **Museo dell'Accademia Etrusca e della Città Cortona,** packed with a wide-ranging collection of Etruscan objects, Renaissance ivories, porcelain, ceramics, miniatures, coins and jewellery. Its highlights are an unusual 5th-century BC Etruscan 'chandelier' and a reconstructed Etruscan tomb.

You should also visit San Niccolò, approached through a little walled garden and dominated by an intriguing double-sided altarpiece by Luca Signorelli. San Domenico has another work by Signorelli, a *Madonna and Saints*, while San Francesco boasts a fine *Annunciation* by Pietro da Cortona. Some way outside the walls stands Santa Maria del Calcinaio, a distinguished but rather austere Renaissance church. A far better destination if you want to stretch your legs is the Fortezza Medicea, a ruined Medici fortress at the top of the town, which offers sensational views across Lake Trasimeno and the Umbrian hills.

www.comunedicortona.it

✚ 139 D6

ℹ Via Nazionale 42 ☎ 0575/630 352

Museo Diocesano

✉ Piazza del Duomo 1 ☎ 0575/62 830 🕐 Apr–Sep daily 10–7; Oct–Mar Tue–Sun 10–5 ✋ Moderate

Museo dell'Accademia Etrusca e della Città Cortona
✉ Palazzo Casali, Piazza Signorelli 19 ☎ 0575/630 415 or 637 235
🕐 Apr–Oct daily 10–7; Nov–Mar Tue–Sun 10–5 ✋ Moderate

MONTALCINO

Lofty Montalcino is one of Tuscany's most pleasing hill towns, with picture-perfect streets, magnificent views and some of the best wine in Italy. A fairy-tale **fortezza** (fortress) dominates the town's southern approaches, begun in 1361 and strengthened by Cosimo I in 1571 after the town had fallen to the Medici (Montalcino was the last town of the Sienese Republic to surrender to Florence). Inside is a little wine bar where you can sample local wines, along with a watchtower and battlements with far-reaching views.

You can also buy wines at the Fiaschetteria Italiana, a pretty, turn-of-the century café in Piazza del Popolo, the town's modest main square. On one side of the square stands the narrow Palazzo dei Priori (1292), on another the graceful arches of a Renaissance loggia. The town's new **Museo Civico** is housed in a monastery annexed to the fresco-filled church of Sant'Agostino. The museum

is full of valuable wooden sculptures and wonderful Gothic and Renaissance paintings.

A few kilometres south of Montalcino lies **Sant'Antimo,** a superb Cistercian abbey in glorious pastoral countryside and reputedly founded by Charlemagne in 832, though most of the present Romanesque building dates from the 12th century. The stunning interior features several finely carved capitals: look for the second column on the right, where the capital shows *Daniel in the Lion's Den.*

www.prolocomontalcino.it

✚ 138 E4

🛈 Costa del Municipio 8 ☎ 0577/849 331

Fortezza

✉ Piazzale della Fortezza ☎ 0577/849 211 🕓 Apr–Oct daily 9–8; Nov–Mar daily 9–6 👋 Castle: free. Tower: moderate; joint ticket with Museo Civico
🍴 Wine and snacks from the *enoteca* (€)

Museo Civico

✉ Via Ricasoli 31 ☎ 0577/846 014 🕓 Tue–Sun 10–1, 2–5:50 (5:40 Sep–Mar) 👋 Moderate

Sant'Antimo

✉ 1km (half a mile) from Castelnuovo dell'Abate ☎ 0577/835 659
🕓 Mon–Sat 10:15–12:30, 3–6:30, Sun 9:15–10:45, 3–6 👋 Free

MONTEPULCIANO

Ancient Montepulciano is the highest of the Tuscan hill towns, gazing down across Lake Trasimeno and Umbria's hazy hills. Strung along a narrow ridge, the town hinges around a single main street – the Corso – a precipitous climb that passes a succession of interesting churches and Renaissance palaces. Look for Palazzo Cocconi (No 70), attributed to Antonio Sangallo; Vignola's Palazzo Tarugi (No 82); and the Palazzo Bucelli (No 73), whose lower walls are studded with ancient Etruscan funerary urns.

Further up the hill you pass Michelozzo's Sant'Agostino, and short detours take you to Santa Lucia and San Francesco. Pop in to the **Museo Civico,** home to a selection of Gothic and Renaissance works, and then recover your breath in the Piazza Grande, the town's main square. Here, the Palazzo Comunale's **tower** provides good views, while at Palazzo Cantucci, you can buy the town's famous red wine, *Vino Nobile di Montepulciano*.

Also here is the Duomo, whose high altar shelters Taddeo di Bartolo's radiant *Assumption* (1401). The baptistery chapel (first on the left) features a font and six bas-reliefs (1340) by Giovanni d'Agostino and a della Robbia terracotta which frames a relief of the *Madonna and Child* attributed to Benedetto da Maiano.

Leave time for the short walk southwest, beyond the town walls, to **San Biagio,** a celebrated Renaissance church (1518–45) designed by Antonio Sangallo the Elder.

www.prolocomontepulciano.it; **www.**comune.montepulciano.si.it

✚ 139 E5

ℹ Piazzale Don Minzoni ☎ 0578/757 341

Museo Civico

✉ Via Ricci 10 ☎ 0578/717 300 🕐 Apr–Oct Tue–Sun 10–1, 3–7; Nov–Mar Tue–Sat 10–1, 3–6 ✋ Moderate

Torre Comunale

✉ Palazzo Comunale, Piazza Grande 1 ☎ 0578/757 442 or 757 034 🕐 Call for times ✋ Inexpensive

San Biagio

✉ Via di San Biagio 14 ☎ None 🕐 Daily 9–12, 3–6 ✋ Free

PIENZA

Pienza owes much of its present appearance to Aeneas Piccolomini, later Pope Pius II, who tried to turn his birthplace into a model Renaissance town. The transformation began in 1459, a year after he became pope, and was overseen by Bernardo Rossellino. Pius died before his dream was realized, and only the cathedral, a papal lodging and a handful of palaces were ever built.

Piazza Pio II is the heart of the town, dominated by the façade of the **Duomo.** The lofty interior – now showing alarming signs of collapse – was inspired by German 'hall churches' Pius had seen on his travels around Europe. The tall windows – another papal whim – were designed to create a flood of light, symbolizing the enlightenment of the age. Pius also commissioned the five beautiful Sienese altarpieces ranged around the walls.

To the right is the **Palazzo Piccolomini,** Pius's palace, with its glorious triple-tiered loggia and gardens providing some breath-taking views. Some rooms are open to the public, notably the papal bedroom and weapon-filled Sala d'Armi. Down the Corso Il Rossellino, just past the Piazza Pio II, is the **Museo Diocesano di Pienza.** It has a beautifully displayed collection of tapestries, manuscripts, silverware, embroidery and Sienese paintings.

Don't miss the Pieve di Corsignano, an ancient parish church five minutes' walk from Pienza.

www.comunedipienza.it

✚ 139 E5

🛈 Piazza Pio II ☎ 0578/749 071, 0578/749 905

Duomo

✉ Piazza Pio II ☎ 0578/749 071 🕐 Daily 8–1, 3–7 ✋ Free

Palazzo Piccolomini

✉ Piazza Pio II ☎ 0578/748 503 🕐 Tue–Sun 10–12:30, 3–6. Closed mid-Nov to mid-Dec ✋ Inexpensive

Museo Diocesano di Pienza

✉ Corso Il Rossellino 30 ☎ 0578/748 379 🕐 Mid-Mar to Oct Wed–Mon 10–1, 3–7; Nov to mid-Mar Sat–Sun 10–1, 3–6 ✋ Moderate

SAN GIMIGNANO

Tuscany's most famous village is a picture of medieval perfection, its famous towers rising above orange-tiled houses. Two superb churches, swathed with frescoes, add to its charm; only the summer's immense crowds detract from the village's appeal. An Etruscan and then a Roman settlement, it enjoyed its heyday during the Middle Ages, when its position, close to trade and pilgrimage routes, brought great prosperity. Family rivalries and the Black Death brought its eventual downfall, and in 1348 the village surrendered itself to the protection of Florence. Thereafter it became a sleepy backwater until the arrival of tourism this century.

A combined San Gimignano ticket gives admission to the Museo Civico, Torre Grossa, Cappella di Santa Fina (Collegiata), Museo Archeologico-Spezieria di Santa Fina and Museo Ornitologico (a museum of stuffed birds south of the Rocca).
www.sangimignano.com

➕ 137 B7

ℹ Piazza del Duomo 1 ☎ 0577/940 008

Collegiata
Best places to see, pages 24–25.

Museo d'Arte Sacra

An arch to the left of the Collegiata leads to San Gimignano's Baptistery, whose loggia is frescoed with an *Annunciation* (1482) by Ghirlandaio and Sebastiano Mainardi. The courtyard here contains the entrance to the Museo d'Arte Sacra, a modest museum with Etruscan remains, a *Madonna and Child* by Bartolo de Fredi, an early wooden Crucifix, exquisite illuminated choir books, and a marble bust of Onofrio di Pietro (1493), a local scholar, by Benedetto da Maiano.

✉ Piazza Pecori ☎ 0577/940 316 🕐 Apr–Oct Mon–Fri 9:30–7:10, Sat 9:30–5:10, Sun 12:30–5:10; Mar, Nov to mid-Jan Mon–Sat 9:30–4:40, Sun 12:30–4:40. Closed late Jan–Feb ✋ Inexpensive. Admission also by combined ticket

Museo Civico/Torre Grossa

San Gimignano's principal museum is entered through a lovely courtyard, with a loggia partly covered in frescoes by Sodoma and Taddeo di Bartolo. After climbing the stairs you can either enter the museum or climb the Torre Grossa.

The museum's first room (downstairs) is the frescoed Sala di Dante, so-called because the poet spoke here in 1300 during a diplomatic mission from Florence. Its highlight is Lippo Memmi's *Maestà* (1317). Stairs lead to the picture gallery with a large salon and several smaller rooms on the right and one tiny stone-walled room to the left. Here are three frescoes (1320) showing a husband and wife playing and taking a shared bath before climbing into bed.

In the other rooms are outstanding paintings by Filippino Lippi, Pintoricchio and Benozzo Gozzoli as well as several polyptychs describing the lives of saints Fina and San Gimignano (two of the village patron saints), and a crucifixion by Coppo di Marcovaldo.

✉ Piazza del Duomo ☎ 0577/990 348 🕐 Tower and museum: Mar–Oct daily 9:30–7; Nov–Feb 10–5:30 ✋ Combined ticket for museum and tower: moderate. Combined ticket for museum, tower, Museo Ornitologico and Galleria d'Arte Moderna e Contemporanea: expensive

Piazza della Cisterna

Most people approach central San Gimignano from Porta San Giovanni in the south. From here Via San Giovanni leads past San Francesco, a deconsecrated Pisan-Romanesque church that now serves as a *cantina* selling the village's celebrated white wine. Be sure to walk to the lovely little garden at the back for superb views. At the end of the street you enter Piazza della Cisterna, one of the village's two linked main squares (the other is Piazza del Duomo). The piazza takes its name from the public cistern (1273) which sits at its heart, though the square is more noteworthy for the various medieval palaces and towers on all sides.

Rocca

A short walk from Piazza del Duomo takes you to the Rocca, San Gimignano's old fortress, built in 1353 on the orders of the Florentines. Two centuries later another Florentine, Cosimo I, ordered its destruction (just one of the original towers survives). Today the ruins enclose a pleasant little park with sweeping views from the old ramparts.

Sant'Agostino

The church of Sant'Agostino, begun in 1298, is best known for Benozzo Gozzoli's chancel frescoes of scenes from the *Life of St Augustine* (1463–7). The striking high altar painting, the *Coronation of the Virgin* (1483), is the work of Piero del Pollaiolo; the frescoes on the *Life of the Virgin* (1356) on the walls of the chapel right of the high altar are by Bartolo di Fredi.

The rear wall contains the Cappella di San Bartolo (on the left as you enter), celebrated for its magnificent altar (1495) by Benedetto da Maiano. Its reliefs depict three miracles by San Bartolo, one of the village patron saints, who is buried in the chapel. The three figures above portray the Theological Virtues; Sebastiano Mainardi's frescoes, to the left, show saints Lucy, Nicholas of Bari and Gimignano, the last holding the town of San Gimignano in his arms. The four half-figures (1318) on the church's left wall, by Mino da Fiesole, are believed to be part of Bartolo's original shrine. On the right (south) wall are several notable frescoes, including a *Madonna and Child with Eight Saints* (1494) by Pier Francesco Fiorentino and *Christ with the Symbols of the Passion* by Bartolo di Fredi.

South of the church in the old Santa Fina convent is the **Museo Archeologico,** with Roman and Etrusan finds and the Spezieria di Santa Fina, a medieval pharmacy.

Sant'Agostino

✉ Piazza Sant'Agostino ☎ None 🕐 Apr–Oct daily 7:30–12, 3–7; Nov–Mar 7:30–12, 3–6 💲 Free

Museo Archeologico

✉ Via Folgore 11 ☎ 0577/940 348 🕐 Apr–Oct Sat–Thu 11–6; Nov–Dec Sat–Thu 10–2. Closed Jan–Mar 💲 Moderate

SIENA

Siena is Italy's loveliest medieval city. Originally
Etruscan, it became a Roman colony and later the
capital of a medieval republic and the principal
rival to Florence. Italy's finest piazza, the Campo,
forms its heart, providing the stage for the Palio, a
famous annual horse race. Here, too, is the Palazzo
Pubblico, home to some of the city's greatest works
of art. Nearby lie the Duomo, one of Italy's greatest
Gothic buildings, and the Museo dell'Opera,
sheltering Duccio's majestic multi-panelled Maestà.
www.terresiena.it

➕ 138 C3

ℹ Piazza del Campo 56 ☎ 0577/280551 ◷ Summer:
Mon–Sat 8:30–7:30, Sun 9–3; winter: Mon–Fri 8:30–6:30,
Sat 8:30–1, Sun 9–3

Duomo

Best places to see, pages 28–29.

Museo dell'Opera del Duomo

This museum occupies part of a half-finished
extension to the cathedral, which would have made
it the largest church in Italy (work was abandoned
following the Black Death in 1348). It opens with
the Gallerie delle Statue, with a tondo by Donatello
in the middle of the room, a *Madonna and Child* by
Jacopo della Quercia and wall statues by Giovanni
Pisano from the cathedral's façade. Upstairs, in a
special room, stands Duccio's *Maestà* (1308–11),
a magnificent work consisting of a vast main
altarpiece and countless tiny panels. Other treats
are the *Madonna dagli Occhi Grossi* (Madonna of
the Large Eyes) and the view from the tower.

www.operaduomo.siena.it

✉ Piazza del Duomo 8 ☎ 0577/283 048 ⏰ Mar–May, Sep–Oct daily 9:30–7:30; Jun–Aug daily 9:30–8; Nov–Feb daily 10–5 💰 Expensive

Palazzo Pubblico

The Palazzo Pubblico's medieval outline dominates the Campo's southern flank. Begun in 1297, it was designed as civic offices and still houses council departments. From its courtyard an entrance leads to the **Torre del Mangia** (102m/632ft; 503 steps), reputedly named after its first bell-ringer, a wastrel whose nickname – the *Mangiaguadagni* – meant 'the eater of profits'. Views from the top are breathtaking. A door to the right of the courtyard leads to the **Museo Civico,** a series of chambers decorated by Siena's leading medieval and Renaissance artists. Some of the city's famous paintings are here, including Simone Martini's exquisite *Maestà* (1315–21) and the series of paintings by Ambrogio Lorenzetti on *Good and Bad Government* (1338). Look for the equestrian portrait of *Guidoriccio da Fogliano*, opposite the *Maestà*, controversially attributed to Martini.

Torre del Mangia

✉ Piazza del Campo 1 ☎ 0577/226 230 ⏰ Mid-Mar to Oct daily 10–7; Nov to mid-Mar 10–4 💰 Expensive
❓ The tower has 388 steps

Museo Civico

✉ Piazza del Campo 1 ☎ 0577/226 230 ⏰ Mid-Mar to Oct daily 10–7; Nov, mid-Feb to mid-Mar daily 10–6:30; Dec to mid-Feb daily 10–5:30 💰 Expensive

Piazza del Campo

Best places to see, pages 36–37.

Pinacoteca Nazionale

Siena's Pinacoteca is one of Italy's finest art galleries, its warren of rooms tracing the development of Sienese painting over some 500 years. A lovely and distinct school, the Sienese painters – notably Duccio – drew their early inspiration from Byzantine art, revelling in gold backgrounds, sumptuous tones and stylized Madonnas. Later artists – Pietro Lorenzetti and Simone Martini in particular – moulded these earlier styles to their own purpose, producing beautifully lyrical paintings whose influence was felt as far afield as England and the Netherlands. The gallery then deals with painters such as Sassetta and Giovanni di Paolo, who took stock of Florentine innovations, blending the traditional Sienese motifs with the new wave of Renaissance thinking. Finally the gallery touches on some of Siena's Mannerist stars.

✉ Palazzo Buonsignori, Via San Pietro 29 ☎ 0577/270 508 🕓 Mon 8:30–1:30, Tue–Sat 8:15–7:15, Sun 8:15–1:15 ✋ Moderate

Sant'Agostino

Begun in 1258, Sant'Agostino's interior was remodelled along Baroque lines by Vanvitelli some 500 years later. The church keeps

very irregular hours, but is well worth visiting for a handful of outstanding paintings. Perugino's *Crucifixion* (1506) occupies the second altar of the right (south) aisle. Alongside it, the Cappella Piccolomini contains an *Adoration of the Magi* (1518) by Sodoma and a 14th-century lunette fresco of the *Madonna and Child with Saints* by Ambrogio Lorenzetti. The Cappella Bichi in the south transept has more frescoes and two monochrome medallions by Luca Signorelli.

✉ Prato di Sant'Agostino ☎ None ⏰ Hours vary, consult tourist office 👆 Free

San Domenico

This vast Gothic church, begun by the Dominicans in 1226, is associated with St. Catherine of Siena, Italy's joint patron saint (with St. Francis). The Cappella delle Volte, right of the entrance, features a contemporary portrait (1414) of the saint, and the Cappella di Santa Caterina (midway down the right aisle) has frescoes of scenes from her life by Sodoma (1526). Her skull is kept in the chapel's altar tabernacle. Left of the chapel is a detached fresco of the *Madonna and Child* by Pietro Lorenzetti, brother of Ambrogio (both

probably died in the plague of 1384). The first chapel to the right of the high altar houses Matteo di Giovanni's triptych of the *Madonna and Child with Saints*. Adorning the high altar are a tabernacle and sculpted angels (1475) by Benedetto da Maiano; the second chapel to its left has a *St. Barbara and Saints* (Matteo di Giovanni's masterpiece) and *Madonna and Child* by Benvenuto di Giovanni.

✉ Piazza San Domenico ☎ None ⏰ Apr–Oct 7–1, 3–6; Nov–Mar daily 9–1, 3–6 👆 Free

San Francesco

A fire in 1655 left San Francesco stripped of all but a few works of art. Surviving fragments include a *Crucifixion* (1331) by Pietro Lorenzetti (first chapel left of high altar) and two graphic frescoes by Pietro and his brother Ambrogio (third chapel). The sacristy has a fine polyptych by Lippo Vanni of the *Madonna and Child with Four Saints* (1370), and at the end of the right (south) aisle is the 14th-century tomb of the Tolomei. Outside the church is the **Oratorio di San Bernardino,** whose beautifully panelled upper chapel has 14 large frescoes by Sodoma, Beccafumi and Girolamo del Pacchia (1496–1518).

✉ Piazza San Francesco ☎ Oratorio 0577/283 048 🕐 Church: daily 9–12, 3–5. Oratorio di San Bernardino: Mar–Oct daily 10:30–1:30, 3–5:30. Closed Nov–Feb 💰 Church: free. Oratorio: inexpensive

Santa Maria della Scala

For almost 800 years this large building opposite the Duomo served as an orphanage and hospital. Following its recent closure there are plans to turn it into a vast cultural centre. More and more of the medieval complex is being opened to the public, revealing superlative works of art hidden from view for centuries. Chief of these is a vast fresco cycle (1444) by Domenico di Bartolo and Vecchietta, whose perfectly preserved panels decorate what until recently was a large hospital ward. The pictures show the foundation and daily life of the medieval hospital. A smaller stone-vaulted chapel, the Sagrestia Vecchia, is decorated with another fresco cycle by Vecchietta, who sculpted the famous high altar statue of the *Risen Christ* in SS Annunziata, the hospital's former church. In the bowels of the building lies the eerie Oratorio di Santa Caterina della Notte, where St Catherine once passed nocturnal vigils.

www.santamaria.comune.siena.it

✉ Piazza del Duomo 2 ☎ 0577/224 828 🕐 Mid-Mar to Oct daily 10:30–6:30; Nov to mid-Mar 10:30–4:30 💰 Expensive 🍴 Shop/café (€)

Santa Maria dei Servi

This outlying church is worth the walk for its works of art and the lovely view of the city from its shady terrace. The first main altar on the right contains the *Madonna di Bordone* (1261) by Coppo di Marcovaldo, a Florentine artist; the last altar on the right features Matteo di Giovanni's *Massacre of the Innocents* (1491). An earlier version of the latter subject by Pietro Lorenzetti occupies the right wall of the second chapel right of the high altar. Other works include *The Adoration of the Shepherds* (1404) by one of Lorenzetti's followers, Taddeo di Bartolo; *Madonna della Misericordia* (1431) by one of Taddeo's pupils, Giovanni di Paolo; and *Madonna del Belvedere* (1363) by Jacopo di Mino.

✉ Piazza Manzoni ☎ None 🕓 Daily 9–12:30, 3–5

🖑 Free

a drive around Chianti

Leave Siena (▶ 118–123) to the north, picking up the SR222 towards Castellina in Chianti (21km/13 miles). From Castellina take the SR429 east to Radda in Chianti (10km/6 miles). Two kilometres (1.2miles) east of Radda at Villa there is an optional scenic circuit to the north (15km/9 miles), via Volpaia. Return to the main road at Villa.

The SR222 is one of the more scenic roads in Chianti, but like many in the region it is fairly twisting, so distances are often a good deal longer than they appear on the map. Both Castellina and Radda are major wine producers, and both have pretty central cores, but their outskirts have been tarnished by new building. Volpaia has an evocative 16th-century castle and several watchtowers.

From Radda head east to Badia a Coltibuono (6km/4 miles) and then drive south on the SP408 to Gaiole in Chianti (5km/3 miles). South of the village (3km/

*2 miles), turn left and follow a lovely minor road past
Castagnoli, Linari and San Gusmé (20km/12 miles). Turn
right on the SS484 to Castello di Brolio (8km/5 miles).*

Badia is part of an abbey complex owned by one of
Chianti's leading producers. You can eat in the restaurant
here (see below for details) or buy wine, honey and virgin
olive oil from the estate shop. Gaiole is an unexceptional
village, but the Castello di Brolio is more appealing: One
of Chianti's oldest vineyards, it has been owned by the
Ricasoli family since 1167. Wine can be bought here also,
and there are occasional organized tours of the winery.

*From Brolio return to Siena (26km/16 miles) on the
SP408 via San Giovanni.*

Distance 110km (68 miles) depending on optional detours
Time Allow a day
Start/end point Siena ✚ 138 C3
Lunch Restaurant (€€) ✉ Badia a Coltibuono ☎ 0577/749424;
www.coltibuono.com 🕐 Closed Jan to mid-Mar and Mon Nov–Apr

VOLTERRA

Volterra commands wide views across eerie grey-brown hills, many riddled with the deposits of alum and alabaster that have long been the region's economic mainstay. Learn more in the Alabaster Museum (Museo Storico dell'Alabastro). The Piazza dei Priori is home to the Palazzo dei Priori (1208–57), known for Orcagna's painting of the *Annunciation* (1383) in the first-floor Sala del Consiglio. Also here is the Torre del Porcellino (Piglet's Tower), named after the carved boar to the right of the top window, and the former Bishops' Palace, part of which is taken up with the **Museo d'Arte Sacra.**

Backing on to Piazza dei Priori is the Piazza del Duomo, site of a Baptistery (closed for restoration) and the Duomo, with Mino da Fiesole's high altar tabernacle and sculpted angels (1471) and a painted background by Benozzo Gozzoli. North is the **Pinacoteca-Museo Civico,** renowned for Rosso Fiorentino's *Descent from the Cross* (1521), and earlier Sienese and Florentine paintings. Look for the *balze*, Volterra's famous eroded cliffs; the Roman theatre and other sights in the town's Archaeolgocial Zone (to the north); and the wealth of Etruscan objects in the **Museo Etrusco Guarnacci.**

www.volterratur.it

✚ 137 C6

ℹ Piazza dei Priori 20 ☎ 0588/86 099

Museo d'Arte Sacra

✉ Via Roma 13 ☎ 0588/86 290 🕔 Mid-Mar to mid-Oct daily 9–1, 3–6; mid-Oct to mid-Mar 9–1 💷 Expensive

Museo Etrusco Guarnacci

✉ Via Don Minzoni 15 ☎ 0588/86 347 🕔 Mid-Mar to Oct daily 9–7; Nov–mid-Mar 9–1:45 💷 Expensive. Joint ticket with Pinacoteca

Pinacoteca-Museo Civico

✉ Palazzo Minucci-Solaini, Via dei Sarti 1 ☎ 0588/87 580 🕔 Mid-Mar to Oct daily 9–7; Nov–mid-Mar 8:30–1:45 💷 Expensive

Index

Acknowledgements

The following photographs are held in the Automobile Association's own photo library (AA World Travel Library) and were taken by these photographers:

Abbreviations for the picture credits are as follows: - (t) top; (b) bottom; (l) left; (r) right; (c) centre; (AA) AA World Travel Library.

4l Calcio in Costume, AA/S McBride; **4c** View from Torre del Mangia, AA/S McBride; **4r** San Lorenzo Church, AA/T Harris; **5l** Vineyards, AA/K Paterson; **5c** Piazza della Cisterna, AA/S McBride; **6/7** Calcio in Costume AA/S McBride; **10** Siena Festival, AA/T Harris; **12** Santa Maria Novella train station, AA/T Harris; **13** Moby Wonder Ferry, AA/T Harris; **17** Telephone Box, AA/M Jourdan; **20/21** View from Torre del Mangia, AA/S McBride; **22** Madonna and Child statue, AA/T Harris; **22/23** Tomba di Lorenzo Duca d'Urbino, AA/T Harris; **24/25t** Museo Civico and Collegiata, AA/R Ireland; **24/25b** Fresco in Collegiata, AA/C Sawyer; **26/27** David statue, AA/S McBride; **27** David statue, AA/K Paterson; **28/29** Duomo, AA/T Harris; **30tl** Uffizi Gallery, AA/C Sawyer; **30bl** Madonna painting, AA; **31** Uffizi Gallery, AA/S McBride; **32tr** Museo Nazionale del Bargello, AA/S McBride; **32b** Museo Nazionale del Bargello courtyard, AA/S McBride; **33** Lion emblem, AA/S McBride; **34/35** Museum do San Marco, AA/C Sawyer; **34** San Marco Church, Sant'Antonino Cloisters, AA/S McBride; **35** San Marco Church 'The Annunciation', AA/C Sawyer; **36/37** Piazza del Campo, AA/J Edmanson; **36** Piazza del Campo couple, AA/T Souter; **38/39** Around Santa Croce Church, AA/S McBride; **39tr** Galileo's Tomb, AA/S McBride; **39c** Santa Croce Church, AA/S McBride; **40c** Duomo and Baptistry, AA/T Harris; **40/41** Campanile, AA/T Souter; **42/43** San Lorenzo Church, AA/T Harris; **45** Ponte Vecchio, AA/C Sawyer; **46/47** Baptistry ceiling, AA/C Sawyer; **47** Baptistry, AA/S McBride; **48** Campanile, AA/S McBride; **49** Campanile, AA/S McBride; **50/51** Santa Maria del Carmine Church, AA/S McBride; **52/53**, Battle of the Centaurs, AA/T Harris; **53** Duomo mosaic, AA/S McBride; **54/55** Duomo cupola, AA/K Paterson; **55** Duomo interior, AA/S McBride; **56** Giardino di Boboli, AA/S McBride; **56/57**, Museo della Antica Casa Fiorentina, AA/C Sawyer; **58** Museo Bardini, AA/C Sawyer; **58/59** Museo di Firenze, AA/J Edmanson; **60** S Miniato al Monte church, AA/C Sawyer; **62/63** Museo dell'Opera del Duomo choirloft, AA/S McBride; **63** Museo dell'Opera del Duomo, AA/S McBride; **64/65** Museo di Storia della Scienza, AA/C Sawyer; **66/67** Church of Orsanmichele, AA/C Sawyer; **66** Church of Orsanmichele fleur-de-lys, AA/C Sawyer; **67** Church of Orsanmichele, AA/T Harris; **68** Palazzo Medici-Riccardi, AA/C Sawyer; **68/69** Palazzo Medici-Riccardi, AA/C Sawyer; **69** Palazzo Medici-Riccardi gardens, AA/B Smith; **70/71t** Palazzo Pitti State Apartment, AA/S McBride; **70/71b** palazzo Pitti, AA/S McBride; **72** Palazzo Pitti Sala di Venere, AA/S McBride; **72/73** Palazzo Vecchio, AA/J Edmanson; **74** Piazza della Signoria statues, AA/C Sawyer; **75** Piazza della Signoria, AA/S McBride; **76/77** Ponte Vecchio, AA/S McBride; **78/79** Santissima Annunziata church, AA/C Sawyer; **80** San Lorenzo Church interior, AA/T Harris; **81** San Lorenzo Church cloisters, AA/B Smith; **83** Santa Maria Novella Church nave, AA/S McBride; **84** Santa Maria Novella Church, AA/T Harris; **85** Santa Maria Novella nuns, AA/ S McBride; **86** San Miniato al Monte Church, AA/C Sawyer; **87** San Miniato al Monte Church pulpit, AA/B Smith; **86/87** Piazza di Santa Trinita, AA/T Harris; **88** Santa Trinita Church, AA/S McBride; **89** Altagnana, AA/C Sawyer; **90** Alpi Apuane village, AA/C Sawyer; **91tr** Barga Duomo pulpit, AA/T Harris; **91b** Barga, AA/T Harris; **92** Marble quarry, AA/K Paterson; **93** Villa Poggio a Caiano, AA/K Paterson; **94** Castelnuovo de Garfagnana, AA/K Paterson; **95** Castelnuovo de Garfagnana tiles, AA/K Paterson; **96** Palazzo Controni-Pfanner, AA/K Paterson; **96/97** Cyclist in Lucca, AA/C Sawyer; **98/99t** Church of S Frediano, AA/C Sawyer; **98/99c** San Frediano Church font, AA/C Sawyer; **99** Church of San Michele, AA/K Paterson; **100/101** Spa Tettuccio garden; AA/K Paterson; **101** Duomo and Leaning Tower, AA/C Sawyer; **102/103** Battistero, AA/C Sawyer; **103** Bacchus Fountain, AA/K Paterson; **104** Viareggio, AA/T Harris; **105** Around San Quirico d'Orcia AA/K Paterson; **106** Abbazia di Monte Oliveto Maggiore, AA/T Harris; **107** San Francisco Church, AA/C Sawyer; **108/109t** Piazza della Repubblica Town Hall, AA/T Harris; **108** Museo Diocesano, AA/T Harris; **108/109b** Montalcino AA/S McBride; **110/111** San Biaggio Church, AA/S McBride; **113** City Wall and Duomo, AA/S McBride; **114** San Gimignano, AA/K Paterson; **116** Piazza della Cisterna, AA/S McBride; **116/117** Piazza della Cisterna, AA/S McBride; **117** Sant' Agostino cloisters, AA/S McBride; **118/119** Duomo, AA/S McBride; **120** Sant Agostino, AA/T Harris; **121** Basilica Cateriniana di San Domenico, AA/T Harris; **123** Santa Maria dei Servi AA/S McBride; **124** Radda Vineyard Chianti, AA/K Paterson; **125** Vineyards near Greve, AA/J Edmanson; **126** Alabaster workshop of Rossi, AA/R Ireland; **127** Around San Quirico d'Orcia AA/K Paterson.

Every effort has been made to trace the copyright holders, and we apologise in advance for any accidental errors. We would be happy to apply the corrections in the following edition of this publication.

132 133 134 135

Firenze
140-141

Torre Pendente,
Pisa
★

Collegiata di
San Gimignano ★

Piazza del Campo,
Siena
★ 138
Duomo di Siena

136 137 139

★ Best places to see

■ Featured sight

☐ Florence

☐ Northern Tuscany

☐ Southern Tuscany

| 0 | 10 km |
| 0 | 5 miles |

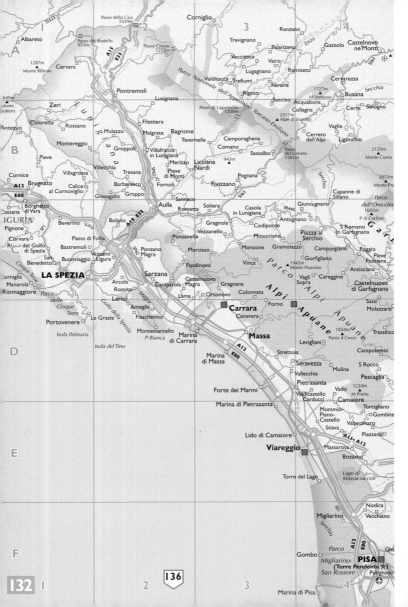

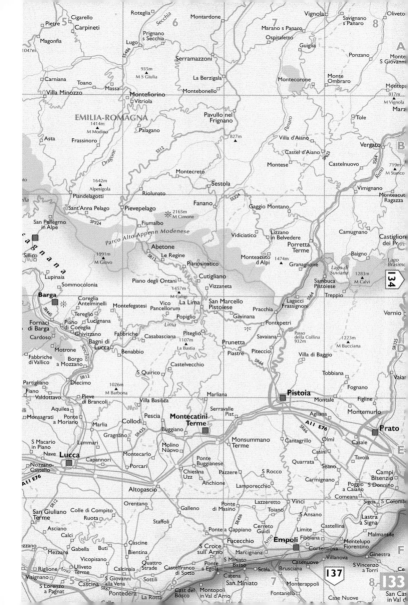

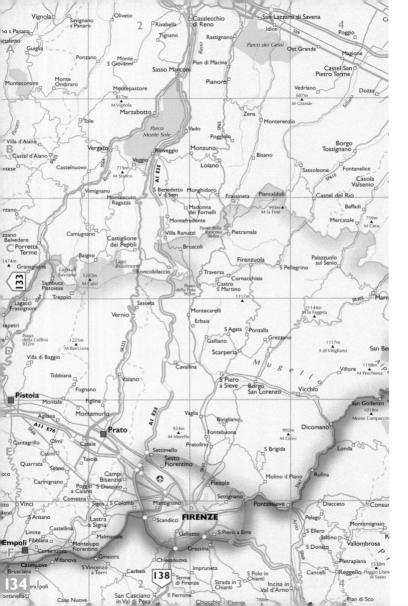

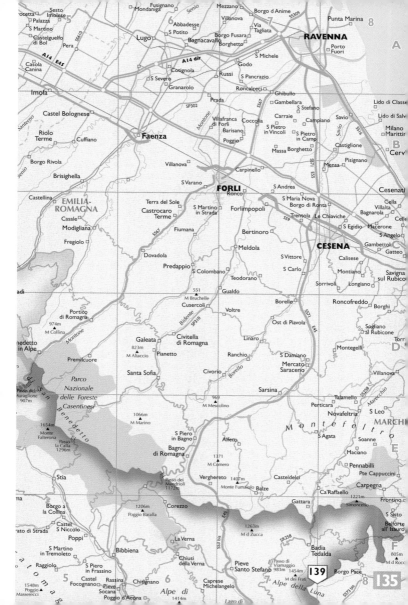

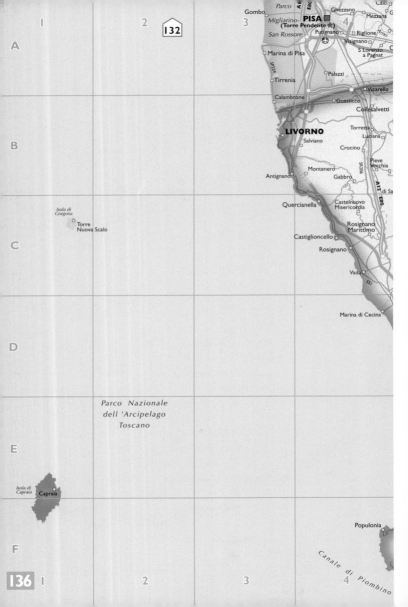

Gombo

Parco

Ghezzano Mezzana Calci

Migliarino- **PISA** ■
(Torre Pendente ★)

Putignano Riglione

San Rossore

Visignano

S Lorenzo a Pagnat

Marina di Pisa

Palazzi

Tirrenia

Vicarello

Calambrone

Guastice

Collesalvetti

LIVORNO

Torretta

Salviano

Luciana

Crocino

Pieve Vecchia

Montenero

Gabbro

Antignano

Quercianella

Castelnuovo Misericordia

Rosignano Marittimo

Castiglioncello

Rosignano

Vada

Marina di Cecina

*Parco Nazionale
dell 'Arcipelago
Toscano*

*Isola di
Gorgona*

Torre
Nuova Scalo

*Isola di
Capraia* Capraia

Populonia

Canale di Piombino

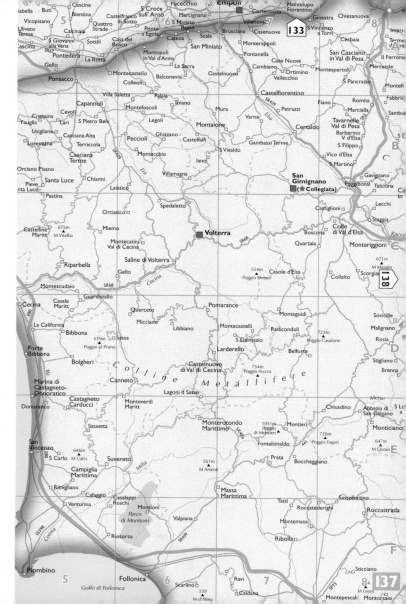

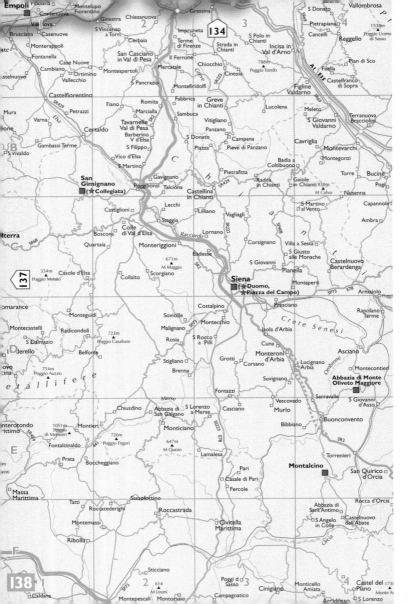

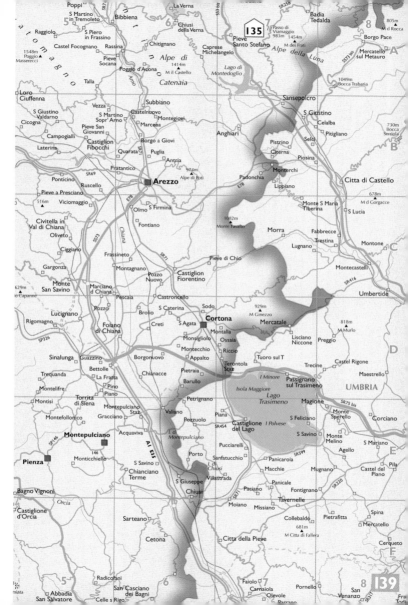

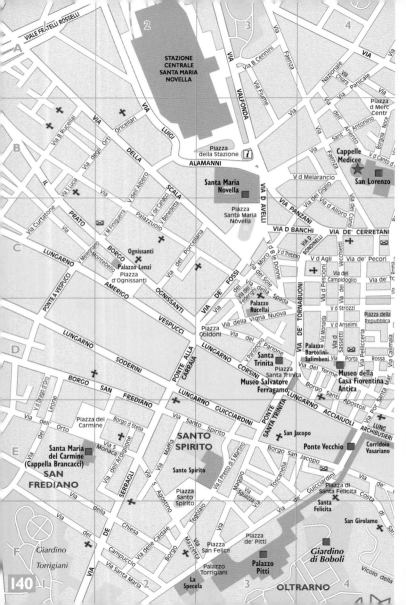

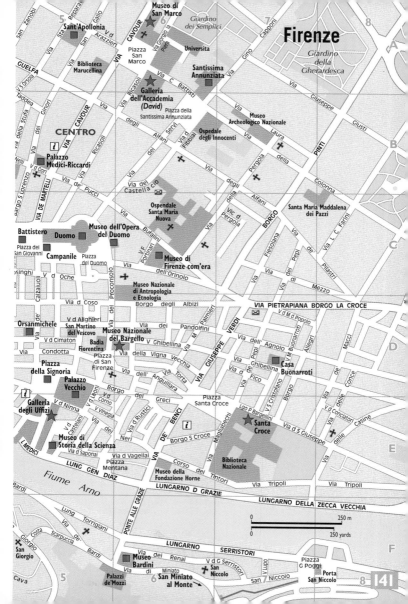

Firenze

Museo di San Marco

Sant'Apollonia

Biblioteca Marucelliana

Giardino dei Semplici

Università

Santissima Annunziata

Galleria dell'Accademia (David)

Piazza San Marco

Piazza della Santissima Annunziata

Giardino della Gherardesca

Museo Archeologico Nazionale

Ospedale degli Innocenti

CENTRO

Palazzo Medici-Riccardi

Santa Maria Maddalena dei Pazzi

Ospendale Santa Maria Nuova

Battistero

Duomo

Museo dell'Opera del Duomo

Campanile

Piazza dei San Giovanni

Piazza del Duomo

Museo di Firenze com'era

Museo Nazionale di Antropologia e Etnologia

Borgo degli Albizi

VIA PIETRAPIANA BORGO LA CROCE

Orsanmichele

San Martino del Vescovo

Badia Fiorentina

Museo Nazionale del Bargello

Piazza di San Firenze

Casa Buonarroti

Piazza della Signoria

Palazzo Vecchio

Galleria degli Uffizi

Piazza Santa Croce

Santa Croce

Museo di Storia della Scienza

Biblioteca Nazionale

Fiume Arno

Museo della Fondazione Horne

Piazza Mentana

LUNG GEN DIAZ

LUNGARNO D GRAZIE

LUNGARNO DELLA ZECCA VECCHIA

0   250 m
0   250 yards

San Giorgio

LUNGARNO SERRISTORI

Museo Bardini

Palazzi de' Mozzi

San Miniato al Monte

San Niccolo

Piazza G Poggi

Porta San Niccolo

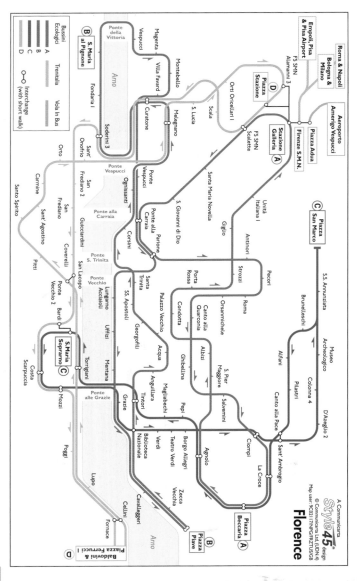

Florence

142